The
Me:
Che....c
Bus Handbook

Counties in this issue:

Cheshire

Merseyside

March 1996

British Bus Publishing

The Merseyside & Cheshire Bus Handbook

The Merseyside and Cheshire Bus Handbook is part of the Bus Handbook series that details the fleets of stage carriage and express coach operators. Where space allows other significant operators in the areas covered are also included. These handbooks are published by *British Bus Publishing* and cover Scotland, Wales and England north of London. The current list is shown at the end of the book. Together with similar books for southern England, published by Capital Transport, they provide comprehensive coverage of all the principal operators' fleets in the British Isles. Handbooks for the FirstBus Group and Stagecoach are also published annually.

The operators included in this edition are those who are based, and provide stage and express services, in the counties of Cheshire and Merseyside. Also included are a number of those operators who provide significant coaching activities.

Quality photographs for inclusion in the series are welcome, for which a fee is payable. The publishers unfortunately cannot accept responsibility for any loss and request you show your name on each picture or slide. Details of changes to fleet information are also welcome.

To keep the fleet information up to date we recommend the Ian Allan publication, Buses published monthly, or for more detailed information, the PSV Circle monthly news sheets. The Staffordshire-based PMT fleet also serve the area using the Crosville name. This fleet will be found in the North & West Midlands Bus Handbook, also part of this series.

The writer and publisher would be glad to hear from readers should any information be available which corrects or enhances that given in this publication.

Series Editor: Bill Potter

Principal Editors: David Donati & Bill Potter

Acknowledgements:
We are grateful to Paul Clayton, Keith Grimes, Martin Grosberg, Mark Jameson, Colin Lloyd, the PSV Circle and the operating companies for their assistance in the compilation of this book.

The cover photographs are by Paul Wigan
Contents correct to February 1996

ISBN 1 890990 14 6
Published by *British Bus Publishing* Ltd
The Vyne, 16 St Margarets Drive, Wellington,
Telford, Shropchiro, TF1 3Г1 I
© British Bus Publishing, March 1996

Contents

A1A TRAVEL

A1A Ltd, 158-164 Price Street, Birkenhead, Merseyside, L41 3PR

1	L1BUS	Mercedes-Benz 609D	North West Coach Sales	B17F	1993	
2	L2BUS	Mercedes-Benz 609D	North West Coach Sales	B17F	1993	
3	M13BUS	Mercedes-Benz 609D	Buscraft	B17F	1995	
4	M4JBA	LDV 400	LDV	M16	1995	
5	SXI9035	Mercedes-Benz L207D	Devon Conversions	M12	1980	Ex BRC, Tockington, 1990
7	AIA9030	Freight Rover Sherpa	Carlyle Citybus 2	B20F	1987	Ex Phil Anslow, Garndiffaith, 1993
8	F452XON	Freight Rover Sherpa	Carlyle Citybus 2	B20F	1988	Ex Midland, 1994
9	L899LFS	Mercedes-Benz 609D	Onyx	C24F	1994	Ex Black, Lochore, 1995
10	AIA5505	Freight Rover Sherpa	Carlyle Citybus 2	B18F	1987	Ex Chesterfield Omnibus, 1994
11	AIA1120	Freight Rover Sherpa	Carlyle Citybus 2	B18F	1987	Ex Chesterfield Omnibus, 1994
12	AIA9000	Mercedes-Benz 709D	Scott	C29F	1991	Ex Skills, Nottingham, 1992
14	E146RNY	Freight Rover Sherpa	Carlyle Citybus 2	B20F	1987	Ex Dalybus, Eccles, 1995
17	OIA773	Bedford CFL	Plaxton Mini Supreme	C17F	1980	Ex Ruxley, Tolworth, 1989
18	OED3W	Mercedes-Benz L508D	Devon Conversions	C18F	1981	Ex Whites of Calver, 1993
20	KGH969A	AEC Routemaster R2RH	Park Royal	H36/28R	1962	Ex London Buses, 1994
21	F430BFY	Mazda E2200	Made-to-Measure	M14	1989	
22	F212AKG	Freight Rover Sherpa	Carlyle Citybus 2	B20F	1988	Ex Shamrock, Pontypridd, 1993
23	PUP565T	Ford R1114	Duple Dominant II	C53F	1979	Ex Walker, Anderton, 1994

Previous Registrations:

AIA1120	E936RWR	AIA9030	E127RAX	OIA773	KBH854V
AIA5505	E933RWR	F430BFY	F636HVM, AIA9000	SXI9035	DFB158W
AIA9000	H62WNN	KGH969A	101CLT		

Livery: Cream and red

Fleet number 10 in the A1A Travel fleet carries an appropriate AIA index mark, AIA5505 and is seen at the Woodside terminus on the Wirral side of the Mersey. One of two former Chesterfield Omnibus Sherpas it carries a Carlyle Citybus 2 body. *Richard Godfrey*

A2B TRAVEL

W G Evans, Prenton Way, North Cheshire Ind Est, Prenton, Merseyside, L43 3DU

KNK369H	Bedford J2SZ10	Plaxton Embassy	C20F	1969	Ex Rothbury Motors, 1995
UIA826	Mercedes-Benz 0303/15R	Mercedes-Benz	C53F	1983	Ex Catteralls, Southam, 1995
A2BDO	Bova FHD12.280	Bova Futura	C49FT	1985	Ex Swallow, Rainham, 1995
D732JUB	Freight Rover Sherpa	Carlyle	B16F	1986	Ex Prince Henry's School, Otley, 1995
D53STJ	Mercedes-Benz L307D	Imperial	M12	1987	Ex Fordies Mini Coaches, Wallasey, 1994
D631RTM	Mercedes-Benz L307D	Reeve Burgess	M12	1987	Ex Time Transport, Thornton Heath, 1992
E56MMT	Mercedes-Benz L307D	Reeve Burgess	M12	1987	Ex Time Transport, Thornton Heath, 1992
E835EUT	Mercedes-Benz L307D	Yeates	M12	1987	Ex Angel, Tottenham, 1994
F130KAO	Mercedes-Benz 609D	Reeve Burgess Beaver	B20F	1989	Ex North Western, 1994
F133KAO	Mercedes-Benz 609D	Reeve Burgess Beaver	B20F	1989	Ex North Western, 1994
F136KAO	Mercedes-Benz 609D	Reeve Burgess Beaver	B20F	1989	Ex North Western, 1994
F223AKG	Iveco Daily 49.10	Carlyle Dailybus 2	DP21F	1988	Ex City Nippy, Middleton, 1995
A2BEO	Mercedes-Benz 609D	Made-to-Measure	C26F	1989	
H506BND	Mercedes-Benz 811D	Made-to-Measure	C19F	1990	
H794HEM	Mercedes-Benz 408D	Made-to-Measure	M15	1991	
H466HBA	Iveco Daily 49.10	Phoenix	B23F	1991	Ex City Nippy, Middleton 1995
L35AKP	Iveco TurboDaily 59.12	Dormobile Routemaker	B27F	1993	
L805YBC	Mercedes-Benz 709D	Dormobile Routemaker	B27F	1993	Ex Kinch, Barrow-on-Soar, 1995
L806YBC	Mercedes-Benz 709D	Dormobile Routemaker	B27F	1993	Ex Kinch, Barrow-on-Soar, 1995
L177PDO	Mercedes-Benz 814D	Autobus Classique	C33F	1993	

Previous Registrations:

A2BDO	B61DMB	A2BEO	G639UHU	UIA826	PUL89Y, ALJ513A

Livery: White, blue and red; black, yellow and white (Merseytravel) L35AKP & H466HBA

Three former North Western minibuses are now with the A2B Travel operation based near West Kirby on the Wirral where the picture was taken. Shown here with Merseytravel service boards is F130KAO which carries a Reeve Burgess Beaver body. *Richard Godfrey*

ABC TRAVEL

D & M Garnett, 7 Rothwell Drive, Ainsdale, Southport, Merseyside, PR8 2SB

Depots: Altcar Road, Fornby; Stephenson Way, Formby

TCK821	Leyland Titan PD3/5	Metro-Cammell	FH41/31F	1963	Ex preservation, 1994
ABC24Y	Leyland Tiger TRCTL11/3RH	Plaxton Paramount 3200 E	C57F	1983	Ex Redline, Penwortham, 1994
ABC75Y	Leyland Olympian ONTL11/2R	Eastern Coach Works	CH45/28F	1983	Ex Clyde Coast, Ardrossan, 1992
D589MVR	Leyland Tiger TRCTL11/3RZ	Plaxton Paramount 3200 III	C53F	1987	Ex Shearings, 1992
F352DVR	Ford Transit VE6	Mellor	B16F	1988	Ex Gascoigne, Partridge Green, 1990
F354DVR	Ford Transit VE6	Mellor	B16F	1988	Ex Gascoigne, Partridge Green, 1990
F203XBV	Freight Rover Sherpa	Carlyle Citybus 2	B20F	1989	
F777GNA	Leyland Tiger TRCTL11/3ARZ	Plaxton Paramount 3200 III	C53F	1989	Ex Shearings, 1993
H4ABC	Optare MetroRider MR01	Optare	B33F	1990	
J55ABC	Mercedes-Benz 709D	Alexander Sprint	DP25F	1991	
J44ABC	Optare MetroRider MR01	Optare	B33F	1992	
J444ABC	Optare MetroRider MR01	Optare	B33F	1992	
J800ABC	DAF SB220LC550	Optare Delta	B49F	1992	Ex Optare demonstrator, 1994
K400ABC	Optare MetroRider MR01	Optare	B33F	1992	
L5ABC	Optare MetroRider MR09	Optare	B22F	1993	
L6ABC	Optare MetroRider MR09	Optare	B22F	1993	
L700ABC	DAF SB220LC550	Optare Delta	B49F	1994	
L99ABC	Mercedes-Benz 709D	Marshall C19	B23F	1994	
L999ABC	Mercedes-Benz 709D	Marshall C19	B23F	1994	
M7ABC	Optare MetroRider MR31	Optare	B24F	1995	
M77ABC	Optare MetroRider MR31	Optare	B24F	1995	
M777ABC	Optare MetroRider MR31	Optare	B24F	1995	
N8ABC	Optare MetroRider MR31	Optare	B24F	1996	
N9ABC	Optare MetroRider MR31	Optare	B24F	1996	
N600ABC	DAF SB220LC550	Northern Counties Paladin	B49F	1996	

Previous Registrations:

ABC24Y	A214DPB		ABC75Y	YPJ503Y, 341AYF, HSB312Y	J800ABC	J365BNW

ABC Travel continue to operate a very modern fleet most of which carry ABC index plates. The latest deliveries are no exception with the newest arrival, a Northern Counties-bodied DAF saloon included on page 99 with the vehicle index at the end of the book. Seen leaving Kirby bus station is J44ABC, one of eleven Optare MetroRiders now operated. *Richard Godfrey*

ACORN TRAVEL

P J Allman, 47 Belgrave Road, Great Boughton, Chester, CH3 5SA
Cheshire Bus & Boat Ltd, Eccleston Ferry Farm, Huntington, Chester, CH3 6EA

Depots: Manor Road, Sealand, Chester

XYJ419	AEC Routemaster R2RH	Park Royal	O36/28R	1961	Ex London Buses, 1995
EGF285B	AEC Routemaster 2R2RH	Park Royal	O36/28R	1964	Ex London Buses, 1995
MCU98K	Leyland Atlantean PDR1A/1Sp	Park Royal	O43/29D	1972	Ex Northumbria, 1994
8795EL	Volvo B58-61	Plaxton Viewmaster III	C53F	1978	Ex Ellerby, Wolsingham, 1994
LEC751X	Bedford YNT	Plaxton Supreme V	C53F	1982	Ex Mullover, Bedford, 1995
UWB534Y	Mercedes-Benz L608D	Reeve Burgess	C25F	1982	Ex Dodd, Sealand, 1995
FIL7290	Ford R1115	Duple Dominant IV	C53F	1983	Ex Highfield, Wigan, 1995
D119WCC	Freight Rover Sherpa	Carlyle	B18F	1987	Ex Crosville Wales, 1992
E137RAX	Freight Rover Sherpa	Carlyle Citybus 2	B20F	1987	Ex McDade, Uddingston, 1995
E150AJC	Freight Rover Sherpa	Carlyle Citybus 2	B20F	1988	Ex Crosville Wales, 1994
F894XOE	Freight Rover Sherpa	Carlyle Citybus 2	B20F	1988	Ex McDade, Uddingston, 1995
F624XDA	Leyland-DAF 400	Leyland DAF	M16	1988	Ex Penny, Cwmgwrach, 1995

Previous Registrations:

8795EL	AUS652S, 12DLY	FIL7290	A568CHH	XYJ419	WLT625
EGF285B	836DYE	MCU98K	JPL110K, WSV572		

Livery: Blue and white; red (Cheshire Bus and Boat), double-deck buses

Acorn use minibuses on services in Chester. Shown here is E150AJC, a Freight Rover Sherpa with Carlyle Citybus 2 bodywork and one previously with Crosville Wales who also operate into this border City. The latest vinyl Cheshire Bus and school bus signs are seen affixed. *Martin Grosberg*

AINTREE COACHLINE

J Cherry, 11 Clare Road, Bootle, Merseyside, L20 9LY

A1	CUL71V	Leyland Titan TNLXB/2RRSp	Park Royal	H44/26D	1980	Ex London Buses, 1994
A2	CUL72V	Leyland Titan TNLXB/2RRSp	Park Royal	H44/26D	1980	Ex London Buses, 1992
A3	ANE2T	Leyland Titan TNLXB/1RF	Park Royal	H47/26F	1979	Ex The Wright Company, Wrexham, 1991
A4	CUL74V	Leyland Titan TNLXB/2RRSp	Park Royal	H44/26D	1980	Ex London Buses, 1994
A5	CUL93V	Leyland Titan TNLXB/2RRSp	Park Royal	H44/26D	1980	Ex London Buses, 1994
A6	HKF151	Leyland Titan TNLXB/2RRSp	Leyland	DPH44/26F	1981	Ex South London, 1995
A7	TMX535R	Leyland Titan B15	Leyland	H44/23F	1977	Ex Universitybus, 1995
A8	HSJ61V	Leyland Atlantean AN68B/1R	Roe	H43/32F	1980	Ex Western Scottish, 1995
L1	F73UJX	Volvo B10M-61	Ikarus Blue Danube	C49FT	1988	Ex Black Prince, Morley, 1995
L2	FIL5123	Volvo B58-61	Plaxton Viewmaster IV	C57F	1980	Ex Abbot Travel, Loanhead, 1995
L3	OHF858S	Leyland National 11351A/1R		DP45F	1978	Ex Merseybus, 1995
L4	BFM293L	Bristol RELH6L	Plaxton Elite III	C47F	1973	Ex Blue Triangle, Bootle, 1993
	TUB250R	Foden-NC/6LXB	Northern Counties	H47/32F	1977	Ex WYPTE, 1989

Previous Registrations:

TMX535R	BCK706R	HKF151	KYV322X, 124CLT, NHM466X
DCM552X	WVR60X, HCK466	LIB4057	WRA28Y
FIL5123	GPD24V, PIA2192, WGA369V		

Livery: Red & cream (buses); gold and red (coaches)

Note: TNX535R is expected to regain the BCK706R mark shortly.

Aintree Coachline have gathered an interesting fleet of vehicles including one of the Foden-NC double-deck buses produced in an association between Northern Counties and former bus producer, Foden. However, here are shown two other types. *Below and opposite top* are views of Titan A5, CUL93V which entered service in dual door configuration and London Buses livery. The addition of several of these Titans has seen the disposal of a former Lancashire United Fleetline pictured here in Aintree Coachline's blue and white livery.
Paul Wigan

ANTHONY'S TRAVEL

A, A, R & D Bamber, Cormorant Drive, Picow Farm Estate, Runcorn, Cheshire WA7 4UD

PIB5898	Aüwaerter Neoplan N116	Aüwaerter Cityliner	C35DT	1981	Ex Goodwin, Eccles, 1995
A288ANT	DAF SB2300DHS585	Jonckheere Jubilee P50	C49FT	1984	Ex Hurst, Wigan, 1994
B262VDB	Peugeot-Talbot Express	Birchall	M14	1984	Ex Birchall, Orford, 1988
LIW6076	Iveco 79.14	Caetano Viana	C19F	1986	Ex East Yorkshire, 1991
D962DWD	Iveco 35.8	Coachcraft	M14	1986	
C652DNE	Peugeot-Talbot Express	Made-to-Measure	M14	1987	Ex Thornton Travel, Widnes, 1992
TIB2387	Bedford YNV Venturer	Duple 320	C50FT	1987	Ex Hurst, Wigan, 1992
E658OCW	Peugeot-Talbot Pullman	Talbot	B20F	1988	Ex Goosecroft, Stirling, 1994
G132ORP	Iveco Daily 49.10	Economy	M15	1990	Ex More-Style, Didsbury, 1995
H146EKM	Leyland-DAF 400	Leyland-DAF	M16	1991	Ex Kent CC, 1995
K555ANT	Leyland-DAF 400	Concept	M16	1993	
K22ANT	Iveco Daily 45.10	Heggie	C18F	1993	Ex Smith, Coupar Angus, 1995
L111ANT	Leyland-DAF 400	Concept	M16	1993	

Previous Registrations:

A288ANT	A383EJS	LIW6076	C158DWT	TIB2387	E800UNB
K22ANT	K12OSB	PIB5898	WGT875W		

Livery: White and red

Anthony's Travel operate PIB5898, a Aüwaerter Neoplan Cityliner integral high floor coach along with a mainly minibus-based operation. Seen in a cream livery, with brown orange and gold relief, the vehicle displays in the windscreen a school bus sign. *Bill Potter*

ARROWEBROOK

A G Parsons, Top Farm, Croughton Road, Croughton, Cheshire, CH2 4DA

OTX59R	Bedford YMT	Caetano Estoril II	C53F	1977	Ex Gouldbourne, Royton, 1981
OFR930T	Bedford YMT	Duple Dominant II	C53F	1979	Ex Battersby-Silver Grey, 1983
HVO17V	Bedford YLQ	Duple Dominant II	C45F	1980	Ex Luxicoaches, Borrowash, 1985
LDM441Y	Mercedes-Benz L508D	Reeve Burgess	C21F	1982	
PTX466Y	Bedford YMP	Duple Dominant IV	C35F	1982	Ex Spratt, Wreningham, 1986
882MMY	DAF MB200DKTL600	Plaxton Paramount 3500	C49FT	1983	Ex Cooper, Killamarsh, 1989
A787PDV	Bedford YMT	Plaxton Paramount 3200	C53F	1984	Ex Snell, Newton Abbott, 1987
B231RRU	DAF SB2305DHS585	Plaxton Paramount 3200 II	C53F	1985	Ex Priory Coaches, Gosport, 1990
D670SEM	Renault-Dodge S56	Northern Counties	B22F	1986	Ex Merseybus, 1993
D672SEM	Renault-Dodge S56	Northern Counties	B22F	1986	Ex Merseybus, 1993
D923PRJ	Freight Rover Sherpa	Made-to-Measure	M16	1987	
E463ANC	Mercedes-Benz 609D	Made-to-Measure	C24F	1988	
F368CHE	Scania K112CRB	Van Hool Alizée	C53FT	1988	Ex Elite, Stockport, 1992
G655EVN	CVE Omni	CVE	DP23F	1990	
G900CRW	Volvo B10M-60	Plaxton Paramount 3500 III	C57F	1990	Ex Harry Shaw, 1994
H434DVM	Mercedes-Benz 609D	Made-to-Measure	C24F	1990	

Previous Registrations:
882MMY   VWB788Y

Livery: White and green

Arrowebrook's D670SEM is seen at the modern Ellesmere Port bus station. One of two former Merseybus Renault-Dodge S56s it carries Northern Counties bodywork is owned. *Paul Wigan*

AVON BUSES

L W Smith, Brook Way, North Cheshire Ind Est, Prenton,
Merseyside, L43 3DT

SDC146H	Leyland Atlantean PDR1A/1	Northern Counties	H43/31F	1970	Ex KHCT, 1995
BNE733N	Daimler Fleetline CRG6LXB	Northern Counties	H43/32F	1974	Ex Merseyline, Garston, 1995
GND502N	Daimler Fleetline CRG6LXB	Northern Counties	H43/32F	1974	Ex Merseyline, Garston, 1995
ANC578A	Ailsa B55-10	Alexander AV	H44/35F	1976	Ex London Buses, 1991
WUH163T	Leyland National 11351A/1R	East Lancs Greenway (1993)	B48F	1978	Ex Rhondda, 1993
CRY33T	Bedford YMT	Plaxton Supreme III	C53F	1979	Ex Happy Al's, Birkenhead, 1995
CUL68V	Leyland Titan TNLXB/2RRSp	Park Royal	H44/26D	1980	Ex London Buses, 1992
CUL91V	Leyland Titan TNLXB/2RRSp	Park Royal	H44/30F	1980	Ex London Buses, 1994
CUL96V	Leyland Titan TNLXB/2RRSp	Park Royal	H44/26D	1980	Ex London Buses, 1992
F112YVP	MCW MetroRider MF158/16	MCW	B28F	1988	Ex Stagecoach East London, 1995

Previous Registrations:
ANC578A   JOV760P

Livery: Blue and cream

BENNETTS

B A Bennett, The Garage, Kerfoot Street, Warrington, Cheshire, WA2 8HU

NTC443M	Bedford YRT	Plaxton Elite III	C53F	1973	Ex Wilkinson, Irlam, 1995
RAW35R	Bedford YLQ	Duple Dominant II	C45F	1977	Ex Tanat Valley, Pentrefelin, 1993
OJV122S	Leyland Fleetline FE30AGR	Roe	H45/29D	1977	Ex Grimsby-Cleethorpes, 1995
JJP335V	Bedford YMT	Duple Dominant II	C53F	1980	Ex Ashton, St Helens, 1987
735JVO	Volvo B10M-61	Van Hool Alizée	C49F	1981	Ex Haldane's of Cathcart, 1995
VJT606V	Ford R1114	Plaxton Supreme V	C53F	1982	Ex Airbus Transfers, Bury, 1995
A450CRM	Mercedes-Benz L608D	Reeve Burgess	C25F	1983	Ex Derek Hilton, Newton-le-Willows, 1995
B854OSB	Dennis Dorchester SDA810	Plaxton Paramount 3500 II	C55F	1985	Ex Western Scottish, 1995
D798KWR	Freight Rover Sherpa	Dormobile	B20F	1987	Ex Yorkshire Rider, 1995
E811JSX	Renault-Dodge S56	Alexander AM	B25F	1987	Ex Clydeside 2000, 1995

Previous Registrations:

735JVO	STT611X		
		B854OSB	B202CGA, VLT272

Livery: White and blue

Avon Buses operate WUH163T in the yellow-based livery of Merseytravel for use on tendered services for that authority. This former Rhondda Leyland National was rebuilt under the East Lancashire Greenway scheme, which is now almost at an end. The picture was taken as the vehicle was entering Heswall bus station heading for West Kirby.
Malc McDonald

F482KFM is one of a pair of Dennis Javelins in the Bostock fleet both of which carry 320 bodywork produced by Duple in 1989. Photographed at the Southport flower show the vehicle is numbered 39. *Paul Wigan*

The sole double-deck with Bostocks is D1, GHM810N, a Daimler Fleetline with MCW bodywork and new to London Transport in 1975. It is seen at the company's Congleton base. *Cliff Beeton*

BOSTOCKS

E J & B Bostock, Spragg Street Garage, Congleton, Cheshire, CW12 1HQ

1	J256MFP	Volvo B10M-60	Plaxton Paramount 3200 III	C57F	1992	
2	VDM937R	Bedford YLQ	Plaxton Supreme III	C45F	1977	
3	UTU550R	Bedford YLQ	Plaxton Supreme III	C45F	1977	
4	JTU228T	Bedford YLQ	Plaxton Supreme III	C45F	1979	
5	WCA942W	Leyland Leopard PSU5D/5R	Plaxton Supreme IV	C57F	1980	
6	SMB601V	Leyland Leopard PSU5D/5R	Duple Dominant II	C57F	1980	
7w	OMB619P	Leyland Leopard PSU5A/4RT	Plaxton Supreme III	C57F	1976	
8	ALG130S	Leyland Leopard PSU5B/4R	Duple Dominant II	C57F	1977	
11	KLG106Y	Bedford YLQ	Plaxton Supreme V	C45F	1982	
12	WCA941W	Leyland Leopard PSU5D/4R	Plaxton Supreme IV	C57F	1980	
14	D437TMB	Bedford YNV Venturer	Duple 320	C53F	1987	
15w	763JTU	Bedford SB1	Plaxton Consort IV	C41F	1960	
16	B847AFM	Bedford YNT	Duple Laser	C53F	1984	
17	F481KFM	Dennis Javelin 12SDA1907	Duple 320	C57F	1989	
19	UTU551R	Leyland Leopard PSU3C/4R	Plaxton Supreme III	C53F	1977	
20	JTU230T	Leyland Leopard PSU5C/4R	Plaxton Supreme IV	C57F	1979	
22	SMB602V	Leyland Leopard PSU5D/5R	Duple Dominant II	C57F	1980	
23	E280XCA	Bedford YMP	Plaxton Paramount 3200 II	C45F	1987	
25	K456PNR	Toyota Coaster HDB30R	Caetano Optimo II	C18F	1992	
26	E281XCA	Bedford YMP	Plaxton Paramount 3200 II	C41F	1987	
27	STU260L	Leyland Leopard PSU5/4RT	Duple Dominant	C57F	1973	
29	JTU226T	Leyland Leopard PSU5C/4RT	Duple Dominant II	C57F	1979	
30	ODM193P	Leyland Leopard PSU3C/4R	Duple Dominant	C53F	1976	
31	A547RCA	Bedford YMP	Plaxton Paramount 3200	C45F	1983	
32	A560RMA	Bedford YNT	Plaxton Paramount 3200	C53F	1983	
33	A818XCA	Bedford YMQ	Plaxton Paramount 3200	C45F	1984	
35	D438TMB	Bedford YNV Venturer	Duple 320	C53F	1987	
36	BCA126W	Leyland Tiger TRCTL11/3R	Duple Goldliner IV	C57F	1981	
38	DCA522X	Bedford YMQ	Plaxton Supreme IV	C41F	1982	
39	F482KFM	Dennis Javelin 12SDA1907	Duple 320	C57F	1989	
40	DFR966W	Leyland Leopard PSU5C/4R	Duple Dominant III	C57F	1980	Ex Leyland Vehicles, 1982
41	F915KCA	Volvo B10M-61	Plaxton Paramount 3500 III	C49F	1989	
42	G956SMB	Volvo B10M-60	Plaxton Paramount 3500 III	C49F	1990	
43	LCA182X	Volvo B10M-61	Duple Goldliner IV	C49FT	1983	
44	LCA183X	Volvo B10M-61	Duple Goldliner IV	C49FT	1983	
45	H621BCA	Volvo B10M-60	Plaxton Paramount 3500 III	C49F	1991	
46	A336WCA	Leyland Tiger TRCTL11/3RH	Duple Caribbean	C49FT	1984	
47	B834CDM	Leyland Tiger TRCTL11/3R	Duple Laser	C51F	1985	
48	F447DUG	Volvo B10M-60	Plaxton Paramount 3500 III	C49FT	1989	Ex Wallace Arnold, 1993
49	F448DUG	Volvo B10M-60	Plaxton Paramount 3500 III	C49FT	1989	Ex Wallace Arnold, 1993
	J692LGA	Volvo B10M-60	Van Hool Alizée	C49FT	1992	Ex Mackies, Alloa, 1995
D1	GHM810N	Daimler Fleetline CRL6	MCW	H44/27D	1975	Ex Smiths, Alcester, 1986

Previous Registrations:

763JTU	From new	J692LGA	J463HDS, LSK504

Livery: Fawn and red.

Note: 49 was the first coach through the Channel Tunnel

Page 13: **Avon Buses'** own livery is white and blue as illustrated here with two examples from the double-deck fleet. The top picture shows CUL91V, one of three Leyland Titans in the fleet while the lower view shows the oldest vehicle in the fleet, SDC146H, a Leyland Atlantean with Northern Counties bodywork from a batch that was new to Cleveland Transit. Both vehicles were undertaking rail replacement duties when pictured. *Paul Wigan*

Overleaf: **Representing the C M T fleet are recently withdrawn 1083, THX166S, a dual-door Leyland National and 2003, a Volvo B10B with Wright Endurance bodywork registered M649YLV.** *Richard Godfrey/Paul Wigan*

C M T

C & M Travel, Unit D3, Liver Industrial Estate, Long Lane, Aintree, Liverpool, L4 7ES

1002w	PTT79R	Leyland National 11351A/1R		B50F	1976	Ex Wingates Tours, Melling, 1993
1022	JBO350N	Leyland National 10351/2R		B44F	1975	Ex Cardiff Bus, 1990
1023	JBO351N	Leyland National 10351/2R		B44F	1975	Ex Cardiff Bus, 1990
1025	BCD803L	Leyland National 1151/1R/0102		B49F	1973	Ex Brighton & Hove, 1989
1028	AYR321T	Leyland National 10351A/2R		B36D	1979	Ex Pennine Blue, 1992
1031	CNB253M	Leyland National 1151/1R/SC		DP48F	1974	Ex Wingates Tours, Melling, 1989
1034	KNH500N	Leyland National 11351/1R		B49F	1975	Ex United Counties, 1990
1035	THX253S	Leyland National 10351A/2R		B36D	1978	Ex Pennine Blue, 1991
1036	HSC110T	Leyland National 11351A/1R		B49F	1978	Ex Wigan Bus Company, 1994
1037	HSC113T	Leyland National 11351A/1R		B49F	1978	Ex Wigan Bus Company, 1994
1038	HSC109T	Leyland National 11351A/1R		B49F	1978	Ex Wigan Bus Company, 1994
1041	HSC112T	Leyland National 11351A/1R		B49F	1978	Ex Wigan Bus Company, 1994
1061	WPT712R	Leyland National 11351A/1R		B49F	1977	Ex Crainey, Kilsyth, 1994
1062	UFG61S	Leyland National 11351A/2R		B44F	1977	Ex Hants & Dorset, 1992
1063	WYJ170S	Leyland National 11351A/2R		B44D	1978	Ex Southdown, 1992
1064	YCD72T	Leyland National 11351A/2R		B44D	1978	Ex Southdown, 1992
1065	GTL359N	Leyland National 11351/1R		B49F	1975	Ex Pennine Blue, 1992
1066	RUF45R	Leyland National 11351A/2R		B44D	1976	Ex Hastings & District, 1992
1067	ABA29T	Leyland National 11351A/1R		B49F	1977	Ex Blue Triangle, Bootle, 1993
1068	YPL413T	Leyland National 10351B/1R		B41F	1978	Ex Blue Triangle, Bootle, 1993
1069	NPK232R	Leyland National 10351A/1R		B41F	1976	Ex County, 1993
1070	LPB221P	Leyland National 10351/1R		B41F	1976	Ex County, 1993
1071	NPK249R	Leyland National 10351A/1R		B41F	1976	Ex County, 1993
1072	SPC266R	Leyland National 10351A/1R		B41F	1977	Ex County, 1993
1073	SPC284R	Leyland National 10351A/1R		B41F	1977	Ex County, 1993
1074	SPC286R	Leyland National 10351A/1R		B41F	1977	Ex County, 1993
1075	SPC291R	Leyland National 10351A/1R		B41F	1977	Ex County, 1993
1076	SPC278R	Leyland National 10351A/1R		B41F	1977	Ex County, 1993
1077	SPC267R	Leyland National 10351A/1R		B41F	1977	Ex County, 1993
1078	LPB222P	Leyland National 10351/1R		B41F	1976	Ex County, 1993
1079	UPB309S	Leyland National 10351A/1R		B41F	1977	Ex County, 1993
1080	UPB317S	Leyland National 10351A/1R		B41F	1977	Ex County, 1993
1081	LPB212P	Leyland National 10351/1R		B41F	1976	Ex County, 1993
1082	UPB308S	Leyland National 10351A/1R		B41F	1977	Ex County, 1993
1084	AKU161T	Leyland National 10351B/1R		B44F	1979	Ex Black Prince, Morley, 1993
1086	BPL477T	Leyland National 10351B/1R		B41F	1979	Ex Sovereign, 1993
1087	AYR303T	Leyland National 10351A/2R		B36D	1978	Ex Dee Ward, Market Harborough, 1993
1088	UHG718R	Leyland National 11351A/1R		B49F	1976	Ex Ribble, 1993
1089	SCK694P	Leyland National 11351A/1R		B49F	1976	Ex Ribble, 1993
1090	SCK696P	Leyland National 11351A/1R		B49F	1976	Ex Ribble, 1993
1091	ERP552T	Leyland National 11351A/1R		B49F	1979	Ex United Counties, 1993
1092	ERP553T	Leyland National 11351A/1R		B49F	1979	Ex United Counties, 1993
1093	ERP555T	Leyland National 11351A/1R		B49F	1979	Ex United Counties, 1993
1094	KRP564V	Leyland National 11351A/1R		B47F	1979	Ex United Counties, 1993
1095	MNH571V	Leyland National 11351A/1R		B49F	1979	Ex United Counties, 1993
1096	MNH576V	Leyland National 11351A/1R		B49F	1979	Ex United Counties, 1993
1097	PJT272R	Leyland National 11351A/1R		B49F	1977	Ex Quickstep, 1994
1098	PEV695R	Leyland National 11351A/1R		B49F	1976	Ex Quickstep, 1994
2001	M647YLV	Volvo B10B	Wright Endurance	B49F	1995	
2002	M648YLV	Volvo B10B	Wright Endurance	B49F	1995	
2003	M649YLV	Volvo B10B	Wright Endurance	B49F	1995	
2004	M650YLV	Volvo B10B	Wright Endurance	B49F	1995	
2005	N652CHF	Dennis Dart 9.8SDL3054	Northern Counties	B40F	1995	
2006	N653CHF	Dennis Dart 9.8SDL3054	Northern Counties	B40F	1995	
2007	N654CHF	Dennis Dart 9.8SDL3054	Northern Counties	B40F	1995	
2008	N655CHF	Dennis Dart 9.8SDL3054	Northern Counties	B40F	1995	
2009	N656CHF	Dennis Dart 9.8SDL3054	Northern Counties	B40F	1995	
2010	N657CHF	Dennis Dart 9.8SDL3054	Northern Counties	B40F	1995	
2011	N658CHF	Dennis Dart 9.8SDL3054	Northern Counties	B40F	1995	

Previous Registrations:
CNB253M   PFM866M, 452WAL

Livery: Red (buses); white and blue (coaches)

CHESTER

Chester City Transport Ltd, Station Road, Chester, CH1 3AD

1	B201EFM	Leyland Olympian ONLXB/1R	Northern Counties	DPH43/30F	1985	
2	B202EFM	Leyland Olympian ONLXB/1R	Northern Counties	DPH43/30F	1985	
3	B203EFM	Leyland Olympian ONLXB/1R	Northern Counties	DPH43/32F	1985	
4	B204EFM	Leyland Olympian ONLXB/1R	Northern Counties	DPH43/32F	1985	
5	VRA124Y	Leyland Olympian ONLXB/1R	Northern Counties	H43/28F	1982	Ex Derby, 1987
6	VRA125Y	Leyland Olympian ONLXB/1R	Northern Counties	H43/28F	1982	Ex Derby, 1987
7	UWW1X	Leyland Olympian ONLXB/1R	Roe	H47/29F	1982	Ex West Yorkshire PTE, 1987
8	UWW2X	Leyland Olympian ONLXB/1R	Roe	H47/29F	1982	Ex West Yorkshire PTE, 1987
9	F209JMB	Leyland Olympian ONCL10/2RZ	Northern Counties	DPH43/32F	1989	
10	F210JMB	Leyland Olympian ONCL10/2RZ	Northern Counties	DPH45/33F	1989	
11	F882VSJ	Leyland Olympian ONCL10/1RZ	Leyland	H47/31F	1988	Ex A1 (McKinnon), Ardrossan, 1991
12	A976OST	Leyland Olympian ONLXB/1R	Alexander RL	H45/30F	1984	Ex Highland Scottish, 1991
13	C378CAS	Leyland Olympian ONLXB/1RH	Alexander RL	H45/30F	1986	Ex Highland Scottish, 1991
14	C379CAS	Leyland Olympian ONLXB/1RH	Alexander RL	H45/30F	1986	Ex Highland Scottish, 1991
15	C380CAS	Leyland Olympian ONLXB/1RH	Alexander RL	H45/30F	1986	Ex Highland Scottish, 1991

16-20
Leyland Lion LDTL11/1R — Alexander RH — DPH49/37F — 1987 — Ex Clydeside 2000, 1994

16	E889CDS	17	E925CDS	18	E941CDS	19	E938CDS	20	E935CDS

24	A157MCK	Leyland Tiger TRCTL11/3R	Duple Dominant IV	C55F	1983	Ex Kirkham, Oswaldtwistle, 1988
25	E25BTU	Dennis Javelin 11SDL1905	Duple 320	C55F	1988	
26	A66KVM	Leyland Tiger TRCTL11/3R	Plaxton Paramount 3200	C55F	1984	Ex GM Buses, 1990
27	A67KVM	Leyland Tiger TRCTL11/3R	Plaxton Paramount 3200	C55F	1984	Ex GM Buses, 1990
28	XFM211	Leyland Tiger TRCTL11/3R	Plaxton Paramount 3200	C55F	1984	Ex GM Buses, 1989
29	E43SBO	Dennis Javelin 11SDA1906	Duple 320	C51F	1988	Ex Bebb, Llantwit Fardre, 1989
30	E126LAD	Hestair Duple SDA1512	Duple 425	C53FT	1988	Ex Swanbrook, Cheltenham, 1993

34-41
Renault-Dodge S56 — Northern Counties — B22F* — 1987-88 — *39-41 are DP23F

34	E134XCA	36	E136XCA	38	E38YFM	40	E40YMB	41	E41YMB
35	E135XCA	37	E137XCA	39	E39YMB				

46	E40PJV	Renault-Dodge S56	Alexander AM	B23F	1988	Ex Grimsby-Cleethorpes, 1989
47	E41PJV	Renault-Dodge S56	Alexander AM	B23F	1988	Ex Grimsby-Cleethorpes, 1989
48	E42PJV	Renault-Dodge S56	Alexander AM	B23F	1988	Ex Grimsby-Cleethorpes, 1989

51-60
Dennis Dart 9SDL3011 — Plaxton Pointer — B35F — 1991-93

51	J51EDM	53	J53EDM	55	J155EDM	57	K57LLG	59	K59LLG
52	J52EDM	54	J54EDM	56	K56LLG	58	K58LLG	60	L160PDM

61	L61PDM	Dennis Dart 9SDL3021	Plaxton Pointer	B35F	1993	
62	L62PDM	Dennis Dart 9SDL3021	Plaxton Pointer	B35F	1993	
63	L63SFM	Dennis Dart 9SDL3031	Plaxton Pointer	B35F	1994	
64	L64SFM	Dennis Dart 9SDL3031	Plaxton Pointer	B35F	1994	
65	M165XMA	Dennis Dart 9SDL3031	Plaxton Pointer	B35F	1994	
66	M166XMA	Dennis Dart 9SDL3031	Plaxton Pointer	B35F	1994	
75	OFM957K	Daimler Fleetline CRG6LX(6LXB)	Northern Counties (1985)	H43/29F	1972	
77	TWH694T	Leyland Fleetline FE30AGR	Northern Counties	H43/32F	1978	Ex GM Buses, 1990
78	HDB124V	Leyland Fleetline FE30AGR	Northern Counties	H43/32F	1980	Ex GM Buses, 1990
79	BCB613V	Leyland Fleetline FE30AGR	Northern Counties	H43/32F	1980	Ex GM Buses, 1990
80	DWH682W	Leyland Fleetline FE30AGR	Northern Counties	H43/32F	1980	Ex GM Buses, 1990

Opposite : **Chester use two distinct liveries for normal service vehicles and the Park & Ride fleet. Seen in traditional cream and maroon is Dennis Dart 63, L63SFM. All the Dennis Darts with Chester are the shorter 9-metre model and carry the Plaxton Pointer body with just 35 seats. Park & Ride vehicles wear a livery of white base and blue and red relief. Shown here is 18, E941CDS, one of five Leyland Lions in the fleet. This model was the mid-engined double deck introduced by Leyland to compete with Volvo's B10MD product, then an increasingly effective competitor.** *Gerry Mead*

Historic Chester provides many attractions for visitors and international tourists to the city. It also benefits from restricted vehicle access - a lesson for many other cities. Offering a tour of the delights is open-top 87, CFM87S here in the joint Chester/Guide Friday scheme with *The Chester Tour* names. *Gerry Mead*

87-98

Leyland Fleetline FE30AGR   Northern Counties   O43/16F* 1978-80   *93/4 are H43/29F

87	CFM87S	92	KFM192T	94	SDM94V	96	SDM96V	98	SDM98V
90	KFM190T	93	KFM193T	95	SDM95V	97	SDM97V		

99-103

Dennis Dominator DD121B   Northern Counties   H43/29F   1981

99	YMA99W	100	YMA100W	101	YMA101W	102	YMA102W	103	YMA103W

104-112

Dennis Dominator DDA150*   Northern Counties   H43/29F   1982-83   *110-112 are DDA170

104	HMA104X	106	HMA106X	108	KLG108Y	110	A110UCA	112	A112UCA
105	HMA105X	107	KLG107Y	109	KLG109Y	111	A111UCA		

121	OCS34X	Dennis Dominator DDA151	East Lancashire	H45/31F	1981	Ex A1 (Duff), Ardrossan, 1988
126	DBV3W	Dennis Dominator DD120	East Lancashire	H43/31F	1981	Ex Warrington, 1989
127w	DBV4W	Dennis Dominator DD120	East Lancashire	H43/31F	1981	Ex Warrington, 1990
129	SCW103X	Dennis Dominator DDA158	East Lancashire	H43/33F	1982	Ex Hyndburn, 1990
130w	SCW104X	Dennis Dominator DDA158	East Lancashire	H43/33F	1982	Ex Hyndburn, 1990
131	A105KRN	Dennis Dominator DDA158	East Lancashire	H43/33F	1983	Ex Hyndburn, 1990
132	A106KRN	Dennis Dominator DDA158	East Lancashire	H43/33F	1983	Ex Hyndburn, 1990
133	B107UFV	Dennis Dominator DDA950	East Lancashire	H43/33F	1985	Ex Hyndburn, 1990
134	B108UFV	Dennis Dominator DDA950	East Lancashire	H43/33F	1985	Ex Hyndburn, 1990
135	JSL282X	Dennis Dominator DD139	East Lancashire	H50/33F	1981	Ex Brighton, 1991
136	JSL283X	Dennis Dominator DD139	East Lancashire	H50/33F	1981	Ex Brighton, 1991
137	JSL284X	Dennis Dominator DD139	East Lancashire	H50/33F	1981	Ex Brighton, 1991
140	MPN140W	Dennis Dominator DD122	East Lancashire	H47/35F	1980	Ex Eastbourne, 1992
141	MPN141W	Dennis Dominator DD122	East Lancashire	H47/35F	1980	Ex Eastbourne, 1992

Previous Registrations:

E880CDS	E100YGD, VLT100	E938CDS	E163YGB, WLT364
E925CDS	E161YGB, FSU661	E941CDS	E162YGB, 32CLT
E935CDS	E164YGB, VLT204	XFM211	A54KVM

Livery: Cream and maroon. white, red and blue (Park & Ride) 1, 2, 18-20; green & cream (Guide Friday/Original Chester Tour) 87, 90/2/5/7; The Liverpool Tour 96, 98.

Four Leyland Olympians from Highland Scottish arrived with Chester in 1991, all carrying Alexander bodywork. Representing the type is 12, A976OST shown in standard livery and pictured while working circular service 6 to Huntington. *Cliff Beeton*

In recent years Chester gathered many second-hand Dennis Dominators into the fleet, the majority with East Lancashire bodywork. The last pair arrived in 1992 from Eastbourne and seen in Northgate Street is 141, MPN141W. *Gerry Mead*

CITY BUS

J C Bleasdale, 99-103, Stanhope Street, Liverpool, L8 5RE

GNJ576N	Bristol VRT/SL2/6LX	Eastern Coach Works	H43/31F	1975	Ex Brighton & Hove, 1990
JJG908P	Leyland National 10351/1R		B41F	1975	Ex East Kent, 1989
EMB370S	Leyland National 11351A/1R		B49F	1978	Ex Crosville Wales, 1991
CWX657T	Leyland National 11351A/1R		B49F	1978	Ex West Riding, 1991
EON830V	Leyland National 2 NL116L11/1R		DP39F	1980	Ex Stevensons, 1992
LUA325V	Leyland National 2 NL106L11/1R		B41F	1980	Ex Stevensons, 1993
LCW731W	Leyland Leopard PSU5D/4R	Plaxton Supreme IV	C57F	1981	Ex Burnley & Pendle, 1994
MEF825W	Bristol VRT/SL3/6LXB	Eastern Coach Works	H43/31F	1981	Ex Northumbria, 1994
SVL174W	Bristol VRT/SL3/6LXB	Eastern Coach Works	H43/31F	1981	Ex RoadCar, 1995
917MMB	Leyland Tiger TRCTL11/3R	Plaxton Supreme V	C53F	1982	Ex Robinsons, Gt Harwood, 1990
JSV343	Aüwaerter Neoplan N722/3	Plaxton Paramount 4000 II	CH53/18CT	1986	Ex Dodsworth, Boroughbridge, 1995
D32MWN	Leyland Lynx LX112TL11ZR1	Leyland Lynx	B51F	1987	Ex Whitelaw, Stonehouse, 1993
D390SGS	Freight Rover Sherpa	Dormobile	B16F	1987	Ex Eagles & Crawford, Mold, 1992
K782VNF	Ford Transit VE6	Deansgate	M14	1992	
L22AJB	Optare MetroRider MR11	Optare	B28F	1994	

Previous Registrations:

917MMB	LEC198X	JSV343	C753CWX	LCW731W	LHE253W, XSU910

Livery: Blue and white.

Two products from the assembly lines at Lillyhall are shown from the City Bus fleet. Opposite top is Leyland Lynx D32MWN which was new to Rees & Williams/West Wales. The lower picture shows Leyland National 2 LUA325V, one of the shorter 10.6-metre examples.
The newest arrival in the City Bus fleet is illustrated below. L22AJB is one of the longer MR11 models of the Optare MetroRider. *Martin Grosberg*

DAVID TANNER TRAVEL

D Tanner, 10 Cowley Street, Haydock, St Helens, Merseyside, WA10 2SR

C531BFB	Ford Transit 190	Dormobile	B16F	1985	Ex Victoria Travel, Earlestown, 1995
C535BHY	Ford Transit 190	Dormobile	B16F	1986	Ex Victoria Travel, Earlestown, 1995
C542BHY	Ford Transit 190	Dormobile	B16F	1986	Ex Victoria Travel, Earlestown, 1995
C567BHY	Ford Transit 190	Dormobile	B16F	1986	Ex Victoria Travel, Earlestown, 1995

David Tanner operates four Ford Transits all of which originated with the Badgerline fleet and with Dormobile bodywork. Shown here is C535BHY. All four were acquired through Victoria Travel who have now ceased operating in favour of dealing. Readers may recall that the earliest NBC minibuses were forecast to have a useful life of some 5-7 years. The large number still running 10-11 years later is testament to their underestimated ruggedness. *Lee Whitehead*

DOBSON'S

Dobson Buses Ltd, 258 Manchester Road, Lostock Gralam,
Northwich, Cheshire, CW9 7PL

Depot: Wincham Park, Chapel Street, Wincham

RWT548R	Bristol VRT/SL3/6LXB	Eastern Coach Works	H43/31F	1976	Ex Yorkshire Rider, 1995
WWO640T	Leyland National 11351A/1R		B49F	1978	Ex Rees & Williams, Tycroes, 1993
FVM741V	Fiat 55.10	Harwin	C25F	1980	Ex Wendy's, Speke, 1995
E898SDW	Renault-Dodge S56	East Lancashire	B29F	1987	Ex Red & White, 1996
F199BCW	Peugeot-Talbot Pullman	Talbot	B20F	1989	Ex Nip-On, St Helens, 1994
G602SJA	Peugeot-Talbot Pullman	Talbot	B22F	1989	Ex Ludlows, Halesowen, 1994
J332LVM	Peugeot-Talbot Pullman	Talbot	B22F	1991	
J387PVR	Peugeot-Talbot Pullman	Talbot	B22F	1992	
L483DOA	Peugeot-Talbot Pullman	TBP	B22F	1993	
N	Iveco TurboDaily 59.12	Mellor	B29F	1996	

Livery: Blue and cream; white(minibuses)

This tri-axle Peugeot-Talbot Pullman of Dobson's is seen on service H44 through Runcorn with part of the famous bridge visible through the trees. The vehicle is L483DOA, one of five of the model operated by Dobson's and this service is operated partly commercially with one Cheshire Bus journey each Saturday. G602SJA was also new to Dobson's, being re-acquired from Ludlows in 1994
Richard Godfrey

EXPRESS TRAVEL

Express Travel Ltd, Woodend Avenue, Speke, Liverpool, L24 9NB

K18AMB	Volvo B10M-60	Plaxton Expressliner II	C46FT	1992
K19AMB	Volvo B10M-60	Plaxton Expressliner II	C40FT	1992
K20AMB	Volvo B10M-60	Plaxton Expressliner II	C46FT	1992
K504WNR	Volvo B10M-60	Plaxton Expressliner II	C46FT	1993
K505WNR	Volvo B10M-60	Plaxton Expressliner II	C46FT	1993
K506WNR	Volvo B10M-60	Plaxton Expressliner II	C46FT	1993
L705PHE	Volvo B10M-62	Van Hool Alizée	C38FT	1994
L706PHE	Volvo B10M-62	Van Hool Alizée	C38FT	1994
L707PHE	Volvo B10M-62	Van Hool Alizée	C38FT	1994
L708PHE	Volvo B10M-62	Van Hool Alizée	C38FT	1994
L709PHE	Volvo B10M-62	Van Hool Alizée	C38FT	1994
L710PHE	Volvo B10M-62	Van Hool Alizée	C38FT	1994
L711PHE	Volvo B10M-62	Van Hool Alizée	C38FT	1994
L712PHE	Volvo B10M-62	Van Hool Alizée	C38FT	1994
L713PHE	Volvo B10M-62	Van Hool Alizée	C38FT	1994
L714PHE	Volvo B10M-62	Van Hool Alizée	C38FT	1994

Livery: Blue, white and red.

After a period in competition with National Express, Express Travel are again working diagrams on the National Express network. Seen passing through Basingstoke while heading home to Southport is L711PHE, a Mark IV Volvo B10M with Van Hool Alizée bodywork and one of four models now approved for the network. *Ralph Stevens*

GRAND EDWARDIAN TOURING COMPANY

C Screaton, Southall Garage, Fennell Street, Warrington, WA1 2PA

FV4548	AEC Regal I	English Electric	C18R	1934	Ex Welsh Historic Trust, Swansea, 1981
KHJ999	AEC Reliance MU3RV	Harrington	C26C	1955	Ex Mulley, Ixworth, 1988
LGV444	AEC Reliance MU3RV	Duple Britannia	C41C	1955	Ex Mulley, Ixworth, 1988
PYM106F	AEC Reliance 6MU3R	Plaxton Panorama I	C30C	1968	Ex Wrigley, Irlam, 198
PYM108F	AEC Reliance 6MU3R	Plaxton Panorama I	C30C	1968	Ex preservation, 1992
B530AYA	MCW Metroliner DR130/6	MCW	CH55/17DT	1985	Ex Sykes, Blackpool, 1995

Livery: Blue and cream

Regal in both looks and marque is FV4548, alias Lord Clive, seen here resplendent at an enthusiasts' rally. Grand Edwardian Touring Company operate five AEC coaches with a variety of period body styles including a Harrington, Duple Britannia and Plaxton Panorama. The original owner of the centre-entrance Paramounts was, of course, Glenton of London, while the AEC Regal was new to Blackpool operator J Salisbury. More prosaically the Metroliner started out with NBC subsidiary Southern National. *Phillip Stephenson*

HALTON

Halton Borough Transport Ltd, Moor Lane, Widnes, Cheshire, WA8 7AF

2 w	MDL880R	Leyland National 11351A/1R		B52F	1976	Ex Southern Vectis, 1987
3 w	ODL884R	Leyland National 10351A/1R		B44F	1977	Ex Southern Vectis, 1987
4 w	ODL883R	Leyland National 10351A/1R		B44F	1977	Ex Southern Vectis, 1987
8	F687YWM	Leyland Lynx LX112L10ZR1	Leyland Lynx	B51F	1988	
9	F81STB	Leyland Lynx LX112L10ZR1	Leyland Lynx	B51F	1989	
11	H34HBG	Leyland Lynx LX2R11C15Z4R	Leyland Lynx	B51F	1991	
13w	YTU983S	Leyland National 11351A/1R		B49F	1977	Ex Crosville, 1987
14	F520AEM	Leyland Lynx LX112L10ZR1	Leyland Lynx	B51F	1989	
15	F521AEM	Leyland Lynx LX112L10ZR1	Leyland Lynx	B51F	1989	
16	F895BKF	Leyland Lynx LX112L10ZR1R	Leyland Lynx	B51F	1989	
17	G221DKA	Leyland Lynx LX2R11C15Z4R	Leyland Lynx	B51F	1989	
19w	ACW919R	Leyland National 11351A/2R		B52F	1977	
21w	ACW921R	Leyland National 11351A/2R		B52F	1977	
22w	BTB22T	Leyland National 11351A/1R		B52F	1979	
23w	BTB23T	Leyland National 11351A/1R		B52F	1979	
24w	BTB24T	Leyland National 11351A/1R		B52F	1979	
25	HED203V	Leyland National NL116L11/1R		B52F	1980	
26	G222DKA	Leyland Lynx LX2R11C15Z4R	Leyland Lynx	B51F	1989	
27	G474DHF	Leyland Lynx LX2R11C15Z4R	Leyland Lynx	B51F	1990	
28	CKC928X	Leyland National 2 NL116AL11/1R		B52F	1982	
29	CKC929X	Leyland National 2 NL116AL11/1R		B52F	1982	
30	EWM630Y	Leyland National 2 NL116TL11/1R		B52F	1983	
31	B131SED	Leyland National 2 NL116TL11/1R		B52F	1985	
32	B132SED	Leyland National 2 NL116TL11/1R		B52F	1985	
33	C49OCM	Leyland National 2 NL116TL11/1R		B52F	1985	
34	D711SKB	Leyland Lynx LX563TL11FR1	Leyland Lynx	B51F	1986	
35	H35HBG	Leyland Lynx LX2R11C15Z4R	Leyland Lynx II	B51F	1990	
36	J249KWM	Leyland Lynx LX2R11C15Z4R	Leyland Lynx II	B51F	1991	
37	J250KWM	Leyland Lynx LX112L10ZR1R	Leyland	B51F	1991	
38	J251KWM	Leyland Lynx LX2R11C15Z4R	Leyland Lynx II	B51F	1991	
40w	ODL886R	Leyland National 10351A/1R		B44F	1977	Ex Southern Vectis, 1987
43	E641VFY	Leyland Lynx LX112TL11ZR1R	Leyland Lynx	B51F	1987	
44	E49WEM	Leyland Lynx LX112L10ZR1	Leyland Lynx	B51F	1988	
45	E642VFY	Leyland Lynx LX112L10ZR1	Leyland Lynx	B51F	1988	

Opposite: **After operating an entirely Lillyhall-assembled fleet, Halton has now added eleven Dennis Darts all of which carry Marshall bodywork. The upper picture shows 60, J923MKC, one of the last of the Leyland Lynx to be delivered while one of the 1996 arrivals from Marshall is seen in Warrington.**
Paul Wigan

Pictured in St George's Place in Liverpool is Halton 29 CKC929X, one of the Leyland National 2s supplied new in 1982. Only one Mark 1 National remains in use though ten are held in reserve.
Richard Godfrey

The off-side view of Lynx 60 is shown in colour while shown here is the same vehicle from the other perspective. Notable is the level entrance step, while some later Lynx bodies featured split level steps. More information on the Lynx is given in The Leyland Lynx Bus Handbook a volume dedicated to the type. *Cliff Beeton*

46	J628LHF	Leyland Lynx LX2R11C15Z4R	Leyland Lynx II	B51F	1992
47	J630LHF	Leyland Lynx LX2R11C15Z4R	Leyland Lynx II	B51F	1992
48	J629LHF	Leyland Lynx LX2R11C15Z4R	Leyland Lynx II	B51F	1992
49	J929MKC	Leyland Lynx LX2R11C15Z4R	Leyland Lynx II	B51F	1992
50	H543FWM	Leyland Lynx LX2R11C15Z4R	Leyland Lynx II	B51F	1990
51	H544FWM	Leyland Lynx LX2R11C15Z4R	Leyland Lynx II	B51F	1990
52	J925MKC	Leyland Lynx LX2R11C15Z4R	Leyland Lynx II	B51F	1992
53	K852MTJ	Leyland Lynx LX2R11C15Z4R	Leyland Lynx II	B51F	1992
54	G473DHF	Leyland Lynx LX2R11C15Z4R	Leyland Lynx	B51F	1990
55	G803EKA	Leyland Lynx LX2R11C15Z4R	Leyland Lynx	B51F	1990
56	H542FWM	Leyland Lynx LX2R11C15Z4R	Leyland Lynx	B51F	1990
57	K853MTJ	Leyland Lynx LX2R11C15Z4R	Leyland Lynx II	B51F	1992
58	J921MKC	Leyland Lynx LX2R11C15Z4S	Leyland Lynx II	B51F	1992
59	J922MKC	Leyland Lynx LX2R11C15Z4S	Leyland Lynx II	B51F	1992
60	J923MKC	Leyland Lynx LX2R11C15Z4R	Leyland Lynx II	B51F	1992
61	J924MKC	Leyland Lynx LX2R11C15Z4R	Leyland Lynx II	B51F	1992
62	J926MKC	Leyland Lynx LX2R11C15Z4R	Leyland Lynx II	B51F	1992
63	J927MKC	Leyland Lynx LX2R11C15Z4R	Leyland Lynx II	B51F	1992
64	J928MKC	Leyland Lynx LX2R11C15Z4R	Leyland Lynx II	B51F	1992

65-78			Dennis Dart 9.8SDL3054		Marshall C37		B40F		1994-96
65	M89DEW	68	M580WLV	71	M583WLV	74	M73AKA	77	N672CLV
66	M87DEW	69	M581WLV	72	M584WLV	75	M74AKA	78	N673CLV
67	M579WLV	70	M582WLV	73	M71AKA	76	N671CLV		

Livery: Red and white

HALTON MINI COACHES

S Williams, 1 Rose Cottage, Northwich Road, Dutton, Runcorn, Cheshire, WA4 4JZ

G966SND	Mazda E2200	Made-to-Measure	M14	1990	
H11JYM	Mercedes-Benz 709D	Reeve Burgess Beaver	B25F	1990	Ex Jim Stones, Glazebury, 1995
H233BBA	Peugeot-Talbot Pullman	Talbot	B22F	1991	Ex Dobson, Lostock Gralam, 1992
H14JYM	Mercedes-Benz 609D	Whittaker	B19F	1991	Ex Jim Stones, Glazebury, 1992

Previous Registrations:
H11JYM   H907SHL

Livery: Silver with black relief

The latest arrival with Halton Mini Coaches is H11JYM, a Mercedes-Benz 709D with Reeve Burgess Beaver bodywork and new to Jim Stones whose *Select* index mark is still carried in this view taken at Runcorn. *Richard Godfrey*

HAPPY AL's

T A Cullinan, 23 Lingham Lane, Moreton, Wirral, Merseyside, L46 7SA

Depot: Corporation Road, Birkenhead

6	CBV15S	Bristol VRT/SL3/501	Eastern Coach Works	H43/31F	1977	Ex Southend, 1992
7	TWS907T	Bristol VRT/SL3/6LXB	Eastern Coach Works	DPH39/27F	1979	Ex Badgerline, 1992
8	AHW204V	Bristol VRT/SL3/6LXB	Eastern Coach Works	H43/30F	1980	Ex City Line, 1993
9	AHW205V	Bristol VRT/SL3/6LXB	Eastern Coach Works	H43/30F	1980	Ex City Line, 1993
10	ALS645V	Bristol VRT/SL3/6LXB	Eastern Coach Works	H43/30F	1980	Ex City Line, 1993
11	AHU520V	Bristol VRT/SL3/6LXB	Eastern Coach Works	H43/30F	1980	Ex City Line, 1993
12	AHU521V	Bristol VRT/SL3/6LXB	Eastern Coach Works	H43/30F	1980	Ex City Line, 1993
13	AHU522V	Bristol VRT/SL3/6LXB	Eastern Coach Works	H43/30F	1980	Ex City Line, 1993
15	A13ALS	Leyland Olympian ONTL11/2R	Eastern Coach Works	CH45/28F	1985	Ex Thamesway, 1991
16	A14ALS	Leyland Olympian ONTL11/2R	Eastern Coach Works	CH45/25F	1985	Ex Thamesway, 1991
17	A9ALS	Leyland Olympian ONLXB/1R	Eastern Coach Works	DPH42/29F	1985	Ex Crosville Wales, 1990
18	A16ALS	Leyland Olympian ONLXB/1R	Eastern Coach Works	DPH42/29F	1985	Ex Crosville Wales, 1990
19	A17ALS	Leyland Olympian ONLXB/1R	Eastern Coach Works	DPH42/29F	1985	Ex Crosville Wales, 1990
20	KJO503W	Bristol VRT/SL3/6LXB	Eastern Coach Works	H43/27D	1980	Ex Oxford Bus Company, 1993
21	KJO506W	Bristol VRT/SL3/6LXB	Eastern Coach Works	H43/27D	1980	Ex Oxford Bus Company, 1993
22	KJO508W	Bristol VRT/SL3/6LXB	Eastern Coach Works	H43/27D	1980	Ex Oxford Bus Company, 1993
23	KJO509W	Bristol VRT/SL3/6LXB	Eastern Coach Works	H43/27D	1980	Ex Oxford Bus Company, 1993
24	PFC511W	Bristol VRT/SL3/6LXB	Eastern Coach Works	H43/27D	1981	Ex Oxford Bus Company, 1993
25	PFC513W	Bristol VRT/SL3/6LXB	Eastern Coach Works	H43/27D	1981	Ex Oxford Bus Company, 1993
26	WAG369X	Leyland Atlantean AN68C/1R	Roe	H43/31F	1982	Ex KHCT, 1994
27	WAG371X	Leyland Atlantean AN68C/1R	Roe	H43/31F	1982	Ex KHCT, 1994
28	WAG372X	Leyland Atlantean AN68C/1R	Roe	H43/31F	1982	Ex KHCT, 1994
29	WAG375X	Leyland Atlantean AN68C/1R	Roe	H43/31F	1982	Ex KHCT, 1994
30	WAG380X	Leyland Atlantean AN68C/1R	Roe	H43/31F	1982	Ex KHCT, 1994
31	WAG382X	Leyland Atlantean AN68C/1R	Roe	H43/31F	1982	Ex KHCT, 1994
	UGB24V	Dennis Dominator DD120B	Willowbrook	H45/33F	1980	Ex Maidstone & District, 1995
	XPT800V	Bristol VRT/SL3/6LXB	Eastern Coach Works	H43/31F	1980	Ex Oare's of Holywell, 1995
	HWJ928W	Bristol VRT/SL3/6LXB	Eastern Coach Works	H43/31F	1980	Ex Avon Buses, Prenton, 1995
	HWJ929W	Bristol VRT/SL3/6LXB	Eastern Coach Works	H43/31F	1980	Ex RoadCar, 1995
	KSD91W	Volvo-Ailsa B55-10	Alexander AV	H44/35F	1980	Ex Clydeside 2000, 1993
	KSD97W	Volvo-Ailsa B55-10	Alexander AV	H44/35F	1980	Ex Avon Buses, Prenton, 1995
	KSD102W	Volvo-Ailsa B55-10	Alexander AV	H44/35F	1980	Ex Avon Buses, Prenton, 1995
	RUA453W	Bristol VRT/SL3/6LXB	Eastern Coach Works	H43/31F	1981	Ex Oare's of Holywell, 1995
	VUA471X	Bristol VRT/SL3/6LXB	Eastern Coach Works	H43/31F	1981	Ex Oare's of Holywell, 1995
	MNS44Y	Dennis Dominator DD162	Alexander RL	H45/34F	1983	Ex Kelvin Central, 1995
	MNS46Y	Dennis Dominator DD162	Alexander RL	H45/34F	1983	Ex Kelvin Central, 1995
	MNS48Y	Dennis Dominator DD162	Alexander RL	H45/34F	1983	Ex Kelvin Central, 1995
	MNS51Y	Dennis Dominator DD162	Alexander RL	H45/34F	1983	Ex Kelvin Central, 1995
	B122NKB	Bova FHD12.280	Bova Futura	C49FT	1985	Ex Crosville Wales, 1990
	C974PFS	Leyland National 2 NL116L11/1R		B52F	1986	Ex Avon Buses, Prenton, 1996
	A18ALS	Leyland Royal Tiger RTC	Leyland Doyen	C53F	1987	Ex Sinclair, Greenhead, 1993
	A19ALS	Leyland Royal Tiger RTC	Leyland Doyen	C53F	1987	Ex Lancaster, 1993
	A20ALS	Aüwaerter Neoplan N122	Aüwaerter Skyliner	CH51/18CT	1987	Ex Express Travel, Perth, 1994
	A10ALS	Leyland Royal Tiger RTC	Leyland Doyen	C53F	1988	Ex West Riding, 1995
	E444MMM	Van Hool T815H	Van Hool Acron	C49FT	1988	Ex Merlyns, Skewen, 1993
	F48ALS	DAF SB2300DHS585	Van Hool Alizée	C51FT	1989	Ex Hurst & Leak, Goose Green, 1993
	H6CLW	Van Hool T815	Van Hool Alizée	C49FT	1991	Ex Warrington, 1994
	H7CLW	Van Hool T815	Van Hool Alizée	C49FT	1991	Ex Warrington, 1994
	N31FWU	DAF DE2LTSB220	Ikarus CitiBus	B48F	1996	
	N32FWU	DAF DE2LTSB220	Ikarus CitiBus	B48F	1996	

Previous Registrations:

A9ALS	C205GTU	A16ALS	C206GTU	ALS645V	AHU518V
A10ALS	E49TYG	A17ALS	C207GTU	B122NKB	B59DMB, A12ALS
A12ALS	-	A18ALS	E44MMT, PJI3749	F48ALS	F272RJX
A13ALS	B692BPU	A19ALS	D457FFG, IIL4012		
A14ALS	B695BPU	A20ALS	E91VWA		

Livery: White, red, orange and yellow.

Opposite: **Happy Al's uses air-brush techniques to apply their graduated yellow to red paint scheme. Illustrating the fleet are a Leyland Royal Tiger with continental-style artwork and Bristol VRT CBV15S, seen outside Lime Street rail station.** *Richard Godfrey/Paul Wigan*

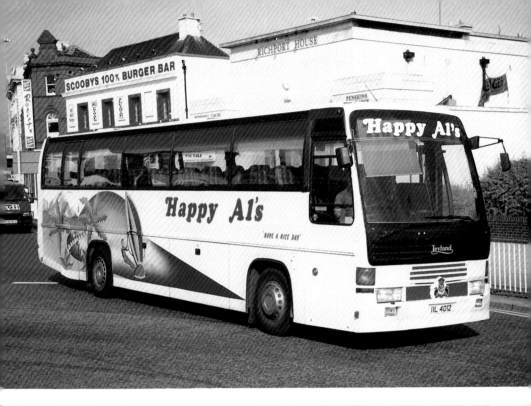

HARDINGS

K & P O'Sullivan, 60 St Johns Road, Huyton, Liverpool, L36 5SY

582WKJ	Aüwaerter Neoplan N122/3	Aüwaerter Skyliner	CH57/20CT	1985	Ex Dixon, Great Harwood, 1993
847XKJ	Scania K112CRS	Van Hool Alizée	C53F	1986	Ex C & G Coaches, Chatteris, 1994
C227EME	Leyland Royal Tiger RT	Van Hool Alizée	C53F	1986	Ex Wingate Travel, 1996
IIL1044	Aüwaerter Neoplan N216H	Aüwaerter Jetliner	C49FT	1987	Ex Wombwell Coaches, 1995
NSU573	Scania K112CRB	Plaxton Paramount 3500 III	C49FT	1987	Ex Goodwin, Stockport, 1993
HPV849	DAF SBR2305DHS570	Van Hool Astrobelle	CH57/14CT	1987	Ex SMC Travel, Garston, 1993
NSU572	LAG G355Z	LAG Panoramic	C49FT	1988	Ex SMC Travel, Garston 1993
E815XKD	Aüwaerter Neoplan N216H	Aüwaerter Jetliner	C49FT	1988	Ex ToppLine, Wavertree, 1995
F819RJF	TAZ D3200	TAZ Tubrava	C49FT	1989	Ex Thandi, Southall, 1989
F379CHE	Scania K92CRB	Duple 320	C55F	1988	Ex C & G Coaches, Chatteris, 1994
F363CHE	Scania K92CRB	Duple 320	C55F	1989	Ex Grange, East Ham, 1990
F600GET	Scania K113CRB	Van Hool Alizée	C55F	1989	Ex Wingate Travel, 1996
G712VRY	TAZ D3200	TAZ Tubrava	C49FT	1990	Ex Bywater, Rochdale, 1991
H399HTJ	Scania K93CRB	Duple 320	C59F	1991	
L401LHE	Scania K113CRB	Van Hool Alizée	C49FT	1994	
L402LHE	Scania K113CRB	Van Hool Alizée	C49FT	1994	
L403LHE	Scania K113CRB	Van Hool Alizée	C49FT	1994	
L973KDT	Toyota Coaster HZB50R	Caetano Optimo III	C21F	1994	
M207PAN	Scania K113CRB	Berkhof Excellence 1000L	C51FT	1994	
M208PAN	Scania K113CRB	Berkhof Excellence 1000L	C51FT	1994	
N205VRX	Volvo B10M-62	Berkhof Excellence 1000L	C51FT	1995	
N206VRX	Volvo B10M-62	Berkhof Excellence 1000L	C51FT	1995	

Previous Registrations:

582WKJ	B888GFT, 92TTT, B385KCU	IIL1044	D808RKY
847XKJ	C158WJU, OO1908, C675WJU	NSU572	E396MVV
E815XKD	E94VWA, TOP11	NSU573	D516SWE
HPV849	E325EVH		

The Hardings fleet is represented by Duple-bodied F379CHE, one of two Scania K92s in the fleet. This example was the first Scania to be bodied by Duple, though not the first into service. Recent bodywork choice at Hardings has been the Dutch-built Berkhof Excellence 1000L which is represented in the fleet on both Volvo B10M and Scania K113CRB. *David Donati collection*

HUXLEY

J F Huxley, Rose Cottage, Greaves Lane East, Threapwood, Malpas,
Cheshire, SY14 7AT

LIL4398	Leyland National 10351/2R		B40D	1975	Ex Orion, Kirkaldy, 1994
LIL2258	Leyland National 11351/1R		B49F	1976	Ex People's Provincial, 1995
LIL4019	Leyland National 10351A/1R		B41F	1977	Ex Northumbria, 1993
UTO3S	Ford R1114	Plaxton Supreme III	C49F	1977	Ex Parish, Hawarden, 1987
YWO182	Ford R1114	Plaxton Supreme III	C40FT	1978	Ex Bee-Line, Middlesbrough, 1983
HIL3931	Ford R1114	Plaxton Supreme III Express	C53F	1978	
HIL3934	Leyland Leopard PSU3E/4R	Duple Dominant I	C49F	1978	Ex Pride of the Road, Royston, 1990
HIL3935	Leyland Leopard PSU3E/4R	Duple Dominant I	C49F	1978	Ex Pride of the Road, Royston, 1990
FUJ937V	Bedford YMT	Duple Dominant II	C53F	1980	Ex Smith, Amble, 1991
YBN632V	Leyland Leopard PSU3E/4R	Plaxton Supreme IV Express	C51F	1980	Ex Aintree Coachline, Bootle, 1992
ESK879	Volvo B10M-61	Van Hool Alizée	C52F	1982	Ex Appleby, Conisholme, 1991
MFE504	Volvo B10M-61	Van Hool Alizée	C46FT	1982	Ex Tellings, Byfleet, 1988
HOI2804	DAF MB200DKFL600	Van Hool Alizée	C50FT	1983	Ex Eniway, Dereham, 1989
B319RJF	Bova EL26/581	Bova Europa	C53F	1984	Ex County, Leicester, 1990
HIL3932	DAF MB200DKVL600	Duple Caribbean	C53F	1986	Ex Happy Days, Woodseaves, 1995
ESK882	DAF MB200DKVL600	Duple Caribbean	C53F	1986	Ex ??, 1995
D120WCC	Freight Rover Sherpa	Carlyle	B18F	1987	Ex Amberline, 1992

Previous Registrations:

B319RJF	B245YKX, 5946PP	HOI2804	KOO760Y
ESK879	VAT222W, AAG275X	LIL2258	KDW338P
ESK882	?	LIL4019	SPC274R
HIL3931	DDM11S	LIL4398	JDT433N, 2749MAN, JDT433N
HIL3932	C459NJX	MFE504	From new
HIL3934	PVB806S	PMB142Y	ANA100Y
HIL3935	PVB807S	YWO182	UUX385S

Livery: Yellow and white or brown and cream.

**Chester Cathedral provides the backdrop to this picture of Huxleys SPC274R, one of three Leyland
Nationals in the fleet all of which now carry marks issued in Northern Ireland.** *Malc McDonald*

JC MINIS

J C Mini Coaches Ltd, Dobson's Coach Yard, Ditton Road, Widnes, Cheshire, WA8 0TH

D846CRY	Volkswagen LT55	Optare City Pacer	B25F	1987	Ex SMC Travel, Garston, 1995
D847CRY	Volkswagen LT55	Optare City Pacer	B25F	1987	Ex SMC Travel, Garston, 1995
D850CRY	Volkswagen LT55	Optare City Pacer	B25F	1987	Ex SMC Travel, Garston, 1995
D852CRY	Volkswagen LT55	Optare City Pacer	B25F	1987	Ex SMC Travel, Garston, 1995
D71WTO	MCW MetroRider MF150/19	MCW	B23F	1987	Ex Stevensons, 1994
D72WTO	MCW MetroRider MF150/20	MCW	B23F	1987	Ex Stevensons, 1994
E801UDT	MCW MetroRider MF150/15	MCW	B23F	1987	Ex Stevensons, 1994
E803UDT	MCW MetroRider MF150/15	MCW	B23F	1987	Ex Stevensons, 1994
E806UDT	MCW MetroRider MF150/15	MCW	B23F	1987	Ex Stevensons, 1994
E807UDT	MCW MetroRider MF150/15	MCW	B23F	1987	Ex Stevensons, 1994
E809UDT	MCW MetroRider MF150/15	MCW	B23F	1987	Ex Stevensons, 1994
E810UDT	MCW MetroRider MF150/15	MCW	B23F	1987	Ex Stevensons, 1994
E763CNL	Peugeot-Talbot Pullman	Talbot	DP22F	1987	Ex Pemberton, Mossley, 1994
E332LHG	Peugeot-Talbot Pullman	Talbot	B17F	1988	Ex Roadrunner, Greenock, 1993
F391DOA	Peugeot-Talbot Pullman	Talbot	B22F	1988	Ex Pathfinder, Newark, 1993
F249HDB	Peugeot-Talbot Pullman	Talbot	B23F	1988	Ex SMC Travel, Garston, 1994
F182JFW	Peugeot-Talbot Pullman	Talbot	B17F	1988	Ex Irwell Valley, Boothstown, 1993
F442DKM	Peugeot-Talbot Pullman	Talbot	B22F	1989	Ex Kent CC, 1994
G391ORR	Peugeot-Talbot Pullman	Talbot	B22F	1989	Ex Pathfinder, Newark, 1993
G146TGX	Peugeot-Talbot Pullman	Talbot	B17F	1990	Ex Transcity, Sidcup, 1993
G147TGX	Peugeot-Talbot Pullman	Talbot	B17F	1990	Ex Transcity, Sidcup, 1993
G148TGX	Peugeot-Talbot Pullman	Talbot	B17F	1990	Ex Transcity, Sidcup, 1993
G569BHP	Peugeot-Talbot Pullman	Talbot	DP20F	1990	Ex North Rider, Cramlington, 1993
H451AGB	Peugeot-Talbot Pullman	Talbot	DP22F	1991	Ex Wilson, Strathaven, 1993
w H392KPY	CVE Omni	CVE	B23F	1990	Ex Trading Post, Herne Bay, 1992

Livery: Merseytravel's black, yellow and white.

Captured on film as it passed through Garston is E809UDT one of several MCW MetroRiders in the fleet which entirely carries the Merseytravel yellow, white and black scheme. Mersey Travel is the non-operation public transport authority which serves the Merseyside Metropolitan County.
Richard Godfrey

JIM STONES COACHES

J Stones, The Jays, Light Oaks Lane, Glazebury, Cheshire, WA3 5LH

Depot: Hope Carr Way, Leigh

TEC599N	AEC Reliance 6MU4R	Plaxton Elite III Express	C45F	1974	Ex Jackson, Kirkby Stephen, 1991
BUS1T	Leyland-DAB 9.948L	DAB	B41F	1984	Ex Leyland Vehicles, 1986
B1BUS	Leyland-DAB Tiger Cub	DAB/Eastern Coach Works	B46F	1985	Ex Tees, 1993
F22TMP	Mercedes-Benz 709D	Reeve Burgess Beaver	B25F	1989	
J5BUS	Mercedes-Benz 709D	Plaxton Beaver	B23F	1991	
J55BUS	Mercedes-Benz 709D	Plaxton Beaver	B27F	1992	
BUS1N	Mercedes-Benz 709D	Plaxton Beaver	B27F	1992	
H1JYM	Mercedes-Benz 709D	Plaxton Beaver	B27F	1993	
L5BUS	Mercedes-Benz 709D	Plaxton Beaver	B27F	1993	
L55BUS	Mercedes-Benz 709D	Plaxton Beaver	B27F	1994	
M1BUS	Mercedes-Benz 709D	Plaxton Beaver	B27F	1996	
M15BUS	Mercedes-Benz 709D	Plaxton Beaver	B27F	1995	
M55BUS	Mercedes-Benz 709D	Plaxton Beaver	B27F	1995	

Previous Registrations:

B1BUS	B500MPY	BUS1T	A499MHG	M1BUS	From new
BUS1N	From new	H1JYM	From new		

Livery: Blue and white

Jim Stones operates local services in the Greater Manchester town of Leigh, though the operation itself is based in Cheshire. Mercedes-Benz minibuses form the majority of the fleet, though the only pair of Leyland-DAB Tiger Cubs are also operated. This model was originally under development as a replacement for the Bristol LH and one of these is pictured on page 102. *Roy Marshall*

LADYLINE COACHES

H Lomas, Mount Pleasant Farm, Key Green, Congleton, Cheshire, CW12 3PZ

UWW525L	Bedford YRT	Plaxton Elite III	C52F	1973	Ex Hollinshead's Cs, Biddulph, 1993
EYL318V	Bedford YMT	Plaxton Supreme IV	C53F	1980	Ex Royal Ordnance, 1991
FBX562W	Bedford YMQ	Duple Dominant	B45F	1980	Ex Knotty Bus, Chesterton, 1994
GIL2403	Bedford YNT	Duple Dominant IV	C53F	1980	Ex Nightingale, Exmouth, 1992
MVM33W	Bedford VAS5	Duple Dominant II	C29F	1980	Ex Crickhowell Coaches, 1993
OPV893W	Bedford CFL	Plaxton Mini Supreme	C17F	1980	Ex Worthington, Collingham, 1985
USE434X	Bedford CFL	Plaxton Mini Supreme	C17F	1982	Ex Trevann, Crawley, 1992
B87CDS	Bedford YNT	Wright Contour	C53F	1985	Ex AAA Coaches, Edinburgh, 1994
B784RNA	Ford Transit 160	Dixon Lomas	C16F	1985	Ex Parker, Leamington, 1993
TJI1696	Volkswagen LT55	Optare City Pacer	B25F	1986	Ex M&H Coaches, Denbigh, 1995

Previous Registrations:

GIL2403	KUX214W	TJI1696	D357JUM

Livery: Cream and red

The not-so-common Wright Contour coach body shown here operated by Ladyline is B87CDS. The Contour was developed from Wright's existing TT bus body and, in styling terms, was rather advancedfor its time. It is possible that, had Wright been as well established in the PCV market as it is now,the Contour may well have interested a wider market. *Paul Wigan*

LOFTY'S

Lofty's Tours Ltd, Morley Bridge, Bridge Trafford, Chester, CH2 4JR

ALG163J	Leyland Leopard PSU4B/4R	Plaxton Elite III	C45F	1971	Ex Hollis Coaches, Sealand, 1993
WVO856S	Bristol LH6L	Eastern Coach Works	DP37F	1977	Ex Bluebird, 1993
C854EML	Volvo B9M-46	Plaxton Bustler	DP33F	1986	Ex Ralphs, Langley, 1995
D51RLG	Mercedes-Benz L608D	PMT Hanbridge	B20F	1986	
F867TNH	Volvo B10M-61	Caetano Algarve	C49FT	1988	Ex Scancoaches, North Acton, 1995
F869TNH	Volvo B10M-61	Caetano Algarve	C49FT	1988	Ex Scancoaches, North Acton, 1995
G27XBK	Iveco Daily 49.10	Phoenix	B25F	1990	
H184CNS	Mercedes-Benz 609D	Made-to-Measure	C19F	1991	
K106RNS	Mercedes-Benz 709D	Dormobile Routemaker	B29F	1993	
L970VGE	Mercedes-Benz 709D	Wadham Stringer Wessex II	B29F	1994	
M878DDS	Mercedes-Benz 709D	Wadham Stringer Wessex II	B29F	1994	
M880DDS	Mercedes-Benz 709D	Wadham Stringer Wessex II	B29F	1994	
N998KUS	Mercedes-Benz 814D	Mellor	C33F	1995	
N941MGG	Mercedes-Benz 709D	Marshall C19	B29F	1995	
N942MGG	Mercedes-Benz 709D	Marshall C19	B29F	1995	
N943MGG	Mercedes-Benz 709D	Marshall C19	B29F	1995	
N935ETU	Iveco TurboDaily 59.12	Mellor	B25F	1995	
N936ETU	Iveco TurboDaily 59.12	Mellor	B25F	1995	
N102EMB	Mercedes-Benz 814D	Crystals	DP31F	1996	

Previous Registrations:
ALG163J   NCK108J, 102UTF

Livery: White or blue and white

Until recently Lofty's operated four Dormobile Routemaker-bodied Mercedes-Benz 709s on their Cheshire Bus services. Caught by the camera at Ellesmere Port bus station was H613CGG which, with its sisters has migrated to Blackpool to new-starter Phoenix handybus. That operator is featured in the Lancashire, Cumbria & Manchester Bus recently published. *Paul Wigan*

MATTHEWS

G Matthews, 15 Deer Park Road, Gayton, Wirral, L60 3RG

Depot: Chester High Road, Neston, Wirral

998AVO	Volvo B10M-61	Jonckheere Bermuda	C51F	1982	Ex McLaughlin, Penwortham, 1995
E75PUH	Freight Rover Sherpa	Carlyle Citybus 2	B20F	1987	Ex Roy Brown, Builth Wells, 1993
E968SVP	Freight Rover Sherpa	Carlyle Citybus 2	B20F	1987	Ex Little White Bus, Ormskirk, 1993
E576UNE	Renault-Dodge S56	Northern Counties	B25F	1988	Ex Thamesdown, 1995
G220EOA	Iveco Daily 49.10	Carlyle Dailybus 2	DP25F	1989	Ex Matthews, Parkgate, 1993

Previous Registrations:
998AVO   DVV523X

Livery: Cream

MERCURY

A J Degnan, Whitchurch Road, Spurstow, Cheshire, CW6 9TD

	D920MVU	Mercedes-Benz 609D	Made-to-Measure	B18FL	1986	Ex City Nippy, Middleton, 1989
	D81BCK	Freight Rover Sherpa	Elme Orion	C16F	1987	Ex Brooklyn, Barnes, 1991
w	D29PVS	Freight Rover Sherpa	Dormobile	B16F	1987	Ex Inverness Traction, 1990
	D223GLJ	Freight Rover Sherpa	Dormobile	B16F	1987	Ex Happy Days, Woodseaves, 1992
w	D139LTA	Renault-Dodge S56	Reeve Burgess Beaver	B23F	1986	Ex Woods, Leicester, 1995
	E270BRG	Renault-Dodge S56	Alexander AM	B19F	1987	Ex Red & White, 1994
	F388CKU	Mercedes-Benz 609D	Whittaker Europa	C24F	1988	Ex West London, Tylers Green, 1992
w	G771FJC	Volkswagen LT55	Optare City Pacer	DP25F	1989	Ex KMP, Llanberis, 1993
w	G774FJC	Volkswagen LT55	Optare City Pacer	DP25F	1989	Ex KMP, Llanberis, 1993
	G214AHP	Peugeot-Talbot Pullman	Talbot	B22F	1990	Ex Transcity, Sidcup, 1993
	H541EVM	Mercedes-Benz 709D	Made-to-Measure	B26F	1991	Ex Woods, Falkirk, 1995

Livery: White and blue

A Volvo chassis forms the base for 998AVO, a Jonckheere Bermuda now in the Matthews fleet. This was the first style from the Jonckheere stable to be imported into Great Britain and has been followed by the Jubilee and Deauville models. This years UK intake will include the Deauville in single-deck and articulated form. *Martin Grosberg*

Mercury operate from a base on the main A49 trunk road with school and tendered services being the main business. Shown here is F388CKU, a Mercedes-Benz 609 with Whittaker Europa bodywork. *Bill Potter*

MEREDITH

JK, ME & DJ Meredith, Lydgate, Well Street, Malpas, Cheshire, SY14 8DE

GUJ356	Bedford OB	Duple Vista	C29F	1950	Ex Mid Wales, Newtown, 1976
SCS363M	Leyland Leopard PSU3/3R	Alexander AY	DP53F	1974	Ex Strathtay Scottish, 1987
SCS365M	Leyland Leopard PSU3/3R	Alexander AY	DP53F	1974	Ex Strathtay Scottish, 1987
852RKN	Leyland Leopard PSU3E/4R	Plaxton Supreme III Express	C53F	1978	Ex Roberts, Aberystwyth, 1989
798MMA	Ford R1114	Plaxton Supreme III	C53F	1978	
510UMA	Ford R1114	Plaxton Supreme III	C53F	1978	
USO187S	Ford R1114	Alexander AYS	B53F	1978	Ex Strathtay Scottish, 1987
RLS468T	Ford R1014	Alexander AYS	B45F	1979	Ex Strathtay Scottish, 1987
EDC406V	Leyland Leopard PSU3E/4R	Plaxton Supreme IV Express	DP53F	1979	Ex Clydeside, 1995
NAX511	Leyland Leopard PSU3F/5R	Plaxton Supreme IV Express	C53F	1980	Ex Evans, Manmoel, 1992
469KHP	Ford R1114	Plaxton Supreme IV	C53F	1980	Ex Bennett, Gloucester, 1994
JED904	Ford R1114	Plaxton Supreme IV	C53F	1981	
884MMB	Volvo B10M-61	Plaxton Paramount 3200	C57F	1983	
122BLM	Volvo B10M-61	Plaxton Paramount 3200 II	C53F	1985	
OLG7	Volvo B10M-61	Plaxton Paramount 3500 III	C49FT	1988	
JCM396	Volvo B10M-60	Plaxton Paramount 3200 III	C53F	1989	
684DYX	Volvo B10M-60	Plaxton Paramount 3200 III	C53F	1989	Ex Applebys, Conisholme, 1993
KSV408	Volvo B10M-61	Plaxton Paramount 3200 III	C57F	1989	Ex Alexander's, Aberdeen, 1992
WAW367	Volvo B10M-60	Plaxton Paramount 3200 III	C53F	1989	Ex Wallace Arnold, 1992
HJI843	Dennis Javelin 12SDA2131	Plaxton Premiére 320	C53F	1995	
	Volvo B10M-62	Plaxton Premiére 320	C53F	1996	

Previous Registrations:

122BLM	From new	HJI843	M472ACA
469KNP	YUO44W	JCM396	F238OFP
510UMA	EDM888S	JED904	WCA893W
684DYX	F511NFW, KRO718, F521RTL	KSV408	F102HSO
798MMA	ATU887S, 2801DK, ETU841S	NAX511	CEP117V
852RKN	VAV986S	OLG7	E400BTU
884MMB	From new	WAW367	F432DUG

Livery: Beige, yellow and red

The latest arrival for the Meredith fleet had still to be registered when the book went to press thought it is expected to will receive a Classic index mark shortly. Pictured at the depot we see the Premier 320 bodied Volvo B10M.
Bill Potter

MERSEYLINE

Meadowhall Ltd, Unit 41 Garston Ind Est, Brunswick Street, Garston, Liverpool, L19 8JB

NOC445R	Leyland Fleetline FE30AGR	MCW	H43/33F	1977	Ex City Fleet, Bootle, 1993
SDA638S	Leyland Fleetline FE30AGR	Park Royal	H43/33F	1977	Ex J C Coaches, Widnes, 1994
SDA564S	Leyland Fleetline FE30AGR	MCW	H43/33F	1978	Ex Rotherham & District, 1993
SDA565S	Leyland Fleetline FE30AGR	MCW	H43/33F	1978	Ex City Fleet, Bootle, 1993
SDA712S	Leyland Fleetline FE30AGR	MCW	H43/33F	1978	Ex West Midlands Travel, 1995
SDA767S	Leyland Fleetline FE30AGR	MCW	H43/33F	1978	Ex City Fleet, Bootle, 1993
SDA768S	Leyland Fleetline FE30AGR	MCW	H43/33F	1978	Ex Amberley Travel, Leeds,1993
SDA772S	Leyland Fleetline FE30AGR	MCW	H43/33F	1978	Ex City Fleet, Bootle, 1993
SDA778S	Leyland Fleetline FE30AGR	MCW	H43/33F	1978	Ex J C Coaches, Widnes, 1994
SDA784S	Leyland Fleetline FE30AGR	MCW	H43/33F	1978	Ex Amberley Travel, Leeds, 1993
TWH703T	Leyland Fleetline FE30AGR	Northern Counties	H43/32F	1978	Ex GMN, 1995
TWH704T	Leyland Fleetline FE30AGR	Northern Counties	H43/32F	1979	Ex GMN, 1995
YTE587V	Leyland Fleetline FE30AGR	Northern Counties	H43/32F	1979	Ex GMN, 1995
BCB617V	Leyland Fleetline FE30AGR	Northern Counties	H43/32F	1980	Ex GMN, 1995
BCB618V	Leyland Fleetline FE30AGR	Northern Counties	H43/32F	1980	Ex GMN, 1995
DWH685W	Leyland Fleetline FE30AGR	Northern Counties	H43/32F	1980	Ex GMN, 1995
E351SWY	Iveco Daily 49.10	Robin Hood City Nippy	DP19F	1988	Ex GMN, 1995
E457TYG	Iveco Daily 49.10	Robin Hood City Nippy	B23F	1988	Ex GMN, 1995

Livery: White and blue

Merseyline have recently taken into stock several Northern Counties-bodied Leyland Fleetlines that have started to displace the older MCW examples similar to SDA772S, seen leaving Liverpool city centre for Garston. *Roy Marshall*

MTL

MTL Trust (Holdings) Ltd, Edge Lane, Liverpool, L7 9LL.
Fareway Passenger Services Ltd, Unit A4 Horn House Lane, Kirkby, Merseyside, L33 7YG
Merseyrider Ltd, Shaw Road, Speke, Liverpool, L24 9JT.
Merseyside Transport Ltd, Edge Lane, Liverpool, L7 9LL
MTL(Heysham) Ltd, Middleton Road, Heysham, Lancashire, LA3 2SE.
MTL London, 17-19 Highgate Hill, London N19 5NA
R&I Tours Ltd, Western Road, Park Royal, London, NW10 7LA

Depots: Laird Street, Birkenhead; Middleton Road, Heysham; Pemberton Gardens, Holloway; Speke Road, Garston, Liverpool; East Lancashire Road, Gillmoss, Liverpool; Green Lane, Liverpool; Woodend Avenue, Speke, Liverpool; Victoria Road, North Acton, London; Western Avenue, Park Royal, London; High Street, Potters Bar; Jackson Street, St Helens and Canning Street, Southport.

0001	WCN643Y	Volvo B10M-56	Van Hool Alizée	C53F	1982	Ex Fairway, 1994
0002	B483UNB	Volvo B10M-61	Van Hool Alizée	C53F	1985	Ex Fairway, 1994
0015	VRG415T	MCW Metrobus DR101/4	MCW	H46/30F	1979	Ex London Buses, 1993
0016	VRG416T	MCW Metrobus DR101/4	MCW	H46/30F	1979	Ex London Buses, 1993
0017	VRG417T	MCW Metrobus DR101/4	MCW	H46/30F	1979	Ex London Buses, 1993
0018	VRG418T	MCW Metrobus DR101/4	MCW	H46/30F	1979	Ex London Buses, 1993
0019	UKA19V	MCW Metrobus DR101/3	MCW	H43/30F	1979	
0020	UKA20V	MCW Metrobus DR101/3	MCW	H43/30F	1980	
0021	UKA21V	MCW Metrobus DR103/2(Gardner)	MCW	H43/30F	1980	
0022	UKA22V	MCW Metrobus DR103/2(Gardner)	MCW	H43/30F	1980	
0023	UKA23V	MCW Metrobus DR103/2(Gardner)	MCW	H43/30F	1980	
0030	ACM704X	Leyland Olympian ONTL11/1R	Eastern Coach Works	H46/31F	1981	
0034	ACM708X	Leyland Olympian ONTL11/1R	Eastern Coach Works	H46/31F	1981	
0040	ACM712X	Leyland Olympian ONTL11/1R	Eastern Coach Works	H46/31F	1982	
0041	ACM772X	Leyland Olympian ONTL11/1R	Eastern Coach Works	H46/31F	1982	
0042	ACM770X	MCW Metrobus DR104/9(Gardner)	Alexander RL	H45/31F	1982	
0043	ACM771X	MCW Metrobus DR104/9(Gardner)	Alexander RL	H45/31F	1982	

0056-0063

		MCW Metrobus DR102/29		Alexander RL		H45/31F	1982	61-63 are DPH45/31F

0056u	EKA156Y	0058	DEM758Y	0060	DEM760Y	0062	DEM762Y	0063	DEM763Y
0057	EKA157Y	0059	DEM759Y	0061	DEM761Y				

0064-0068

		Leyland Olympian ONTL11/1R	Alexander RL	DPH43/25F 1983

0064	A316GLV	0065	A317GLV	0066	A318GLV	0067	A319GLV	0068	A320GLV

0082	A102SUU	Volvo B55-10	Alexander RV	H47/31D	1984	Ex London Northern, 1995
0083	A101SUU	Volvo B55-10	Alexander RV	H47/31D	1984	Ex London Northern, 1995
0093	H838GLD	Mercedes-Benz 609D	North West Coach Sales	B22F	1990	
0094	H839GLD	Mercedes-Benz 609D	North West Coach Sales	B22F	1990	
0095	G922EKF	Mercedes-Benz 609D	North West Coach Sales	B24F	1990	
0096	F373HMB	Mercedes-Benz 609D	North West Coach Sales	C19F	1989	
0097	F68GTU	Mercedes-Benz 609D	North West Coach Sales	C19F	1989	
0098	A863TCA	Mercedes-Benz L608D	Coachcraft	C21F	1983	Ex Ball, St Helens, 1989
0099	E685UVR	Mercedes-Benz 609D	North West Coach Sales	C19F	1988	
0134	PRJ493R	Daimler Fleetline CRG6LXB	Northern Counties	H47/32F	1976	Ex Cambus, 1989

159-168

		Leyland Olympian ONCL10/2RZ	Northern Counties	H51/34F	1988

159	F438AKB	161	F440AKB	163	F442AKB	165	F456BKF	167	F458BKF
160	F439AKB	162	F441AKB	164	F455BKF	166	F457BKF	168	F459BKF

172	E913KYR	Leyland Olympian ONLXB/1RH	Northern Counties	H43/30F	1988	Ex London Buses, 1991
173	E926KYR	Leyland Olympian ONLXB/1RH	Northern Counties	H43/30F	1988	Ex London Buses, 1991
174	E916KYR	Leyland Olympian ONLXB/1RH	Northern Counties	H43/30F	1988	Ex London Buses, 1991
175	E928KYR	Leyland Olympian ONLXB/1RH	Northern Counties	H43/30F	1988	Ex London Buses, 1991
193	B693BPU	Leyland Olympian ONTL11/2RH	Eastern Coach Works	CH45/28F	1985	Ex Liverbus, 1995
194	B694BPU	Leyland Olympian ONTL11/2RH	Eastern Coach Works	CH45/28F	1985	Ex Liverbus, 1995

The MTL fleet services several operations from Heysham Travel in the north to MTL London and R&I in the south. The former London vehicles are in the process of being numbered into the integrated system, though not all new numbers have been allocated. Shown in the latest MTL Fareway scheme is 162, F441AKB, a Northern Counties-bodied Leyland Olympian while below is 234, F234YTJ with Merseybus names. Generally, where fleet number-plates are fitted, leading zeros are shown while they are mostly omitted when transfers are used. *Richard Godfrey/Paul Wigan*

A long association with Alexander continued in 1988 with the delivery of fifteen bodies followed by a further batch the next year. Shown here is a near-side picture of 218, E218WBG in Merseybus livery.

0201-215

Leyland Olympian ONCL10/1RZ Northern Counties H45/30F 1988

0201	E201WBG	0204	E204WBG	0207	E207WBG	0210	E210WBG	0214	E214WBG
0202	E202WBG	0205	E205WBG	0208	E208WBG	0212	E212WBG	0215	E215WBG
0203	E203WBG	0206	E206WBG	0209	E209WBG	0213	E213WBG		

0216-0230

Leyland Olympian ONCL10/1RZ Alexander RL H45/30F 1988

0216	E216WBG	0219	E219WBG	0222	E222WBG	0225	E225WBG	0228	E228WBG
0217	E217WBG	0220	E220WBG	0223	E223WBG	0226	E226WBG	0229	E229WBG
0218	E218WBG	0221	E221WBG	0224	E224WBG	0227	E227WBG	0230	E230WBG

0231-0250

Leyland Olympian ONCL10/1RZ Alexander RL H45/30F 1989

0231	F231YTJ	0235	F235YTJ	0239	F239YTJ	0243	F243YTJ	247	F247YTJ
0232	F232YTJ	0236	F236YTJ	0240	F240YTJ	0244	F244YTJ	248	F248YTJ
0233	F233YTJ	0237	F237YTJ	0241	F241YTJ	0245	F245YTJ	249	F249YTJ
0234	F234YTJ	0238	F238YTJ	0242	F242YTJ	0246	F246YTJ	250	F250YTJ

0251-0270

Leyland Olympian ONCL10/1RZ Northern Counties H47/30F 1989

0251	F251YTJ	0255	F255YTJ	0259	F259YTJ	0263	F263YTJ	0267	F267YTJ
0252	F252YTJ	0256	F256YTJ	0260	F260YTJ	0264	F264YTJ	0268	F268YTJ
0253	F253YTJ	0257	F257YTJ	0261	F261YTJ	0265	F265YTJ	0269	F269YTJ
0254	F254YTJ	0258	F258YTJ	0262	F262YTJ	0266	F266YTJ	0270	F270YTJ

0271-0308

Volvo Olympian YN2RV18Z4 Northern Counties Palatine II H47/30F 1995-96

0271	N271CKB	0278	N278CKB	0286	N286CKB	0294	N294CKB	0302	N302CKB
0272	N272CKB	0279	N279CKB	0287	N287CKB	0295	N295CKB	0303	N303CKB
0273	N273CKB	0281	N281CKB	0288	N288CKB	0296	N296CKB	0304	N304CKB
0274	N274CKB	0282	N282CKB	0289	N289CKB	0297	N297CKB	0305	N305CKB
0275	N275CKB	0283	N283CKB	0291	N291CKB	0298	N298CKB	0306	N306CKB
0276	N276CKB	0284	N284CKB	0292	N292CKB	0299	N299CKB	0307	N307CLV
0277	N277CKB	0285	N285CKB	0293	N293CKB	0301	N301CKB	0308	N308CLV

During 1993-94 Busways provided Leyland Fleetlines for the MTL fleet which displaced older Leyland Atlanteans. Currently allocated to the Fairway operation is 404, VCU404T seen here in South St Johns Street in Liverpool. *Paul Wigan*

0360	C375CAS	Leyland Olympian ONLXB/1R	Alexander RL	DPH45/27F	1984	Ex Liverbus, 1995
0361	C376CAS	Leyland Olympian ONLXB/1R	Alexander RL	DPH45/27F	1984	Ex Liverbus, 1995
0362	C377CAS	Leyland Olympian ONLXB/1R	Alexander RL	H45/27F	1984	Ex Liverbus, 1995

0368-0405

| | | Leyland Fleetline FE30AGR | MCW | H43/32F | 1979 | Ex Busways, 1993-94 |

0368	VCU368T	0378	VCU378T	0387	VCU387T	0394	VCU394T	0399	VCU399T
0369	VCU369T	0379	VCU379T	0389	VCU389T	0395	VCU395T	0401	VCU401T
0374	VCU374T	0381	VCU381T	0390	VCU390T	0396	VCU396T	0403	VCU403T
0375	VCU375T	0384	VCU384T	0391	VCU391T	0397	VCU397T	0404	VCU404T
0376	VCU376T	0385	VCU385T	0392	VCU392T	0398	VCU398T	0405	VCU405T
0377	VCU377T	0386	VCU386T	0393	VCU393T				

507	A507GPC	Leyland Olympian ONTL11/2R	Eastern Coach Works	CH45/28F	1984	Ex Aintree Coachline, 1995
DMS2168	OJD168R	Daimler Fleetline CRL	MCW	H44/26D	1978	Ex London Northern, 1994
D2556	THX556S	Leyland Fleetline FE30AGR	Park Royal	O44/27D	1978	Ex London Northern, 1994
630	MCN30K	Leyland-NGT	MCCW/NGT Tynesider	H39/29F	1972	Ex preservation
655	NMY655E	AEC Routemaster R2RH	Park Royal	H32/24F	1967	On extended loan
659	FVY411	AEC Regal III 6821A	Roe(1962)	B39F	1951	On extended loan

701-709

| | | Scania N112DRB | | Alexander RH | H47/33F | 1989 | Ex London Northern, 1994 |

| 701 | F421GWG | 703 | F423GWG | 705 | F425GWG | 707 | F427GWG | 709 | F429GWG |
| 702 | F422GWG | 704 | F424GWG | 706 | F426GWG | 708 | F428GWG | | |

710-721

| | | Scania N113DRB | | Alexander RH | H47/31F | 1991 | Ex London Northern, 1994 |

710	J810HMC	S13	J813HMC	S16	J816HMC	S18	J818HMC	S20	J820HMC
711	J811HMC	S14	J814HMC	S17	J817HMC	S19	J819HMC	S21	J821HMC
S12	J812HMC	S15	J815HMC						

801-825

| | | | | | | | | MCW Metrobus DR132 | MCW | | H46/31F | 1989 | 801-3/5 fitted with Gardner engines |

MCW Metrobus DR132   MCW   H46/31F   1989   801-3/5 fitted with Gardner engines
801-5/16-25 are type DR132/16, 806-15 DR132/17

801	F801YLV	806	F806YLV	811	F811YLV	816	F816YLV	821	F821YLV
802	F802YLV	807	F807YLV	812	F812YLV	817	F817YLV	822	F822YLV
803	F803YLV	808	F808YLV	813	F813YLV	818	F818YLV	823	F823YLV
804	F804YLV	809	F809YLV	814	F814YLV	819	F819YLV	824	F824YLV
805	F805YLV	810	F810YLV	815	F815YLV	820	F820YLV	825	F825YLV

826	E452SON	MCW Metrobus DR102/63	MCW	H45/30F	1987	Ex Great Yarmouth, 1995
827	E453SON	MCW Metrobus DR102/63	MCW	H45/30F	1987	Ex Great Yarmouth, 1995
828	E455SON	MCW Metrobus DR102/63	MCW	H45/30F	1987	Ex Great Yarmouth, 1995

1001-1070

Leyland Atlantean AN68D/1R   Alexander AL   H43/32F   1983-84

1001	A321GLV	1015	A335GLV	1029	A109HLV	1043	A123HLV	1057	A137HLV
1002	A322GLV	1016	A96HLV	1030	A110HLV	1044	A124HLV	1058	A138HLV
1003	A323GLV	1017	A97HLV	1031	A111HLV	1045	A125HLV	1059	A139HLV
1004	A324GLV	1018	A98HLV	1032	A112HLV	1046	A126HLV	1060	A140HLV
1005	A325GLV	1019	A99HLV	1033	A113HLV	1047	A127HLV	1061	A141HLV
1006	A326GLV	1020	A100HLV	1034	A114HLV	1048	A128HLV	1062	A142HLV
1007	A327GLV	1021	A101HLV	1035	A115HLV	1049	A129HLV	1063	A143HLV
1008	A328GLV	1022	A102HLV	1036	A116HLV	1050	A130HLV	1064	A144HLV
1009	A329GLV	1023	A103HLV	1037	A117HLV	1051	A131HLV	1065	A145HLV
1010	A330GLV	1024	A104HLV	1038	A118HLV	1052	A132HLV	1066	A146HLV
1011	A331GLV	1025	A105HLV	1039	A119HLV	1053	A133HLV	1067	A147HLV
1012	A332GLV	1026	A106HLV	1040	A120HLV	1054	A134HLV	1068	A148HLV
1013	A333GLV	1027	A107HLV	1041	A121HLV	1055	A135HLV	1069	A149HLV
1014	A334GLV	1028	A108HLV	1042	A122HLV	1056	A136HLV	1070	B926KWM

1125-1155

Leyland Atlantean AN68A/1R   Northern Counties   H43/32F   1976-77 Ex Liverbus, 1995

1125	ONF675R	1132	SRJ732R	1137	SRJ754R	1143	ONF693R	1149	SRJ742R
1126	ONF678R	1134	SRJ749R	1139	ONF658R	1144	RJA723R	1153	UNA788S
1128	ONF694R	1135	SRJ752R	1140	ONF670R	1146	UNA763S	1155	BNC935T
1131	SRJ731R	1136	SRJ753R	1141	ONF671R	1148	UNA776S		

1201-1210

Volvo Olympian YN2RV18Z4   Northern Counties Palatine II H47/25D   1993   Ex Liverbus, 1995

1201	L201SKD	1203	L203SKD	1205	L205SKD	1207	L207SKD	1209	L209SKD
1202	L202SKD	1204	L204SKD	1206	L206SKD	1208	L208SKD	1210	L210SKD

1211	L211SBG	Volvo Olympian YN2RV18Z4	Northern Counties Palatine II H47/29F	1993	Ex Liverbus, 1995

1212-1219

Volvo Olympian YN2RV18Z4   Northern Counties Palatine II H47/25D   1994-95 Ex Liverbus, 1995

1212	L212TWM	1214	L214TWM	1216	L216TWM	1218	M218YKC	1219	M219YKC
1213	L213TWM	1215	L215TWM	1217	L217TWM				

Liverbus joined the MTL group in 1995 and one of its contributions was a trio of Olympians from the Highland Scottish operation. Interestingly, others from the batch operate with Chester. Still carrying the old livery and number is 361, C376CAS.
Malc McDonald

1300-1392   Leyland Atlantean AN68/1R   Alexander AL   H43/32F   1972-73

1300	DKC300L	1307	DKC307L	1311	DKC311L	1360	DKC360L	1378	DKC378L
1301	DKC301L	1308	DKC308L	1313	DKC313L	1361	DKC361L	1391	DKC391L
1305	DKC305L	1309	DKC309L	1329	DKC329L	1369	DKC369L	1392	DKC392L
1306	DKC306L	1310	DKC310L	1342	DKC342L				

1449-1535   Leyland Atlantean AN68/1R   Alexander AL   H43/32F*   1973-74   *1449, 1524 are O43/32F

1449	GKA449L	1477	GKA477L	1489	GKA489M	1501	GKA501M	1516	GKA516M
1454	GKA454L	1479	GKA479L	1490	GKA490M	1507	GKA507M	1517	GKA517M
1457	GKA457L	1480	GKA480L	1491	GKA491M	1508	GKA508M	1518	GKA518M
1460	GKA460L	1482	GKA482L	1492	GKA492M	1511	GKA511M	1524	GKA524M
1461	GKA461L	1486	GKA486M	1493	GKA493M	1513	GKA513M	1529	GKA529M
1472	GKA472L	1488	GKA488M	1498	GKA498M	1515	GKA515M	1535	GKA535M
1473	GKA473L								

1551-1612   Leyland Atlantean AN68/1R   Alexander AL   H43/32F*   1974   *1551, 1612 are O43/32F

1551	OLV551M	1588	GKA13N	1592	GKA17N	1597	GKA22N	1602	GKA27N
1555	PKB555M	1589	GKA14N	1595	GKA20N	1600	GKA25N	1610	GKA35N
1585	RKA589N	1590	GKA15N	1596	GKA21N	1601	GKA26N	1612	GKA37N
1587	GKA12N								

1626-1685   Leyland Atlantean AN68/1R   Alexander AL   H43/32F   1976

1626	HTJ626P	1632	HTJ632P	1639	HTJ639P	1649	HTJ649P	1669	HTJ669P
1627	HTJ627P	1634	HTJ634P	1642	HTJ642P	1654	HTJ654P	1670	HTJ670P
1628	HTJ628P	1635	HTJ635P	1643	HTJ643P	1655	HTJ655P	1674	HTJ674P
1630	HTJ630P	1636	HTJ636P	1644	HTJ644P	1658	HTJ658P	1682	HTJ682P
1631	HTJ631P	1637	HTJ637P	1646	HTJ646P	1664	HTJ664P	1685	HTJ685P

1687-1724   Leyland Atlantean AN68/1R   East Lancashire   H43/32F   1976

1687	JWM687P	1696	JWM696P	1703	JWM703P	1713	JWM713P	1721	JWM721P
1689	JWM689P	1698	JWM698P	1704	JWM704P	1714	JWM714P	1722	JWM722P
1693	JWM693P	1700	JWM700P	1705	JWM705P	1715	JWM715P	1723	JWM723P
1694	JWM694P	1701	JWM701P	1706	JWM706P	1717	JWM717P	1724	JWM724P
1695	JWM695P	1702	JWM702P	1710	JWM710P	1720	JWM720P		

1726-1764   Leyland Atlantean AN68A/1R   East Lancashire   H43/32F   1976-77

1726	LKF726R	1736	LKF736R	1743	LKF743R	1750	LKF750R	1758	MTJ758S
1727	LKF727R	1737	LKF737R	1744	LKF744R	1751	LKF751R	1759	MTJ759S
1728	LKF728R	1738	LKF738R	1745	LKF745R	1752	LKF752R	1760	MTJ760S
1730	LKF730R	1740	LKF740R	1747	LKF747R	1753	LKF753R	1761	MTJ761S
1731	LKF731R	1741	LKF741R	1748	LKF748R	1754	LKF754R	1762	MTJ762S
1734	LKF734R	1742	LKF742R	1749	LKF749R	1755	LKF755R	1764	MTJ764S
1735	LKF735R								

The older maroon-based livery of Merseybus is now being replaced by the new. Shown here is 1694, JWM694P, a 1976 model of the East Lancashire-bodied Atlantean.
Paul Wigan

MerseyRider names feature in this view of 1717, JWM717P, a Leyland Atlantean with East Lancashire bodywork. The first side window on this batch was lowered to allow for a side destination, the effect being visible in this view. *Richard Godfrey*

1821-1842

Leyland Atlantean AN68A/1R		East Lancashire		H45/33F* 1979-80		*1840 is H43/32F			

1821	RBG821T	1825	RBG825T	1829	TWM213V	1835	TWM219V	1840	RBG840T
1822	TWM209V	1826	RBG826T	1830	TWM214V	1836	TWM220V	1841	RBG841T
1823	TWM210V	1827	RBG827T	1832	TWM216V	1837	RBG837T	1842	TWM221V
1824	TWM211V	1828	TWM212V	1833	TWM217V	1839	RBG839T		

1847	WWM924W	Leyland Atlantean AN68B/1R	Willowbrook	DPH45/39F 1980

1873-1967

Leyland Atlantean AN68B/1R		Alexander AL		H43/32F		1981-82			

1873	XEM873W	1892	XEM892W	1912	XEM912W	1931	ACM731X	1950	ACM750X
1874	XEM874W	1893	XEM893W	1913	ACM713X	1932	ACM732X	1951	ACM751X
1875	XEM875W	1894	XEM894W	1914	ACM714X	1933	ACM733X	1952	ACM752X
1876	XEM876W	1895	XEM895W	1915	ACM715X	1934	ACM734X	1953	ACM753X
1877	XEM877W	1896	XEM896W	1916	ACM716X	1935	ACM735X	1954	ACM754X
1878	XEM878W	1897	XEM897W	1917	ACM717X	1936	ACM736X	1955	ACM755X
1879	XEM879W	1898	XEM898W	1918	ACM718X	1937	ACM737X	1956	ACM756X
1880	XEM880W	1899	XEM899W	1919	ACM719X	1938	ACM738X	1957	ACM757X
1881	XEM881W	1900	XEM900W	1920	ACM720X	1939	ACM739X	1958	ACM758X
1882	XEM882W	1902	XEM902W	1921	ACM721X	1940	ACM740X	1959	ACM759X
1883	XEM883W	1903	XEM903W	1922	ACM722X	1941	ACM741X	1960	ACM760X
1884	XEM884W	1904	XEM904W	1923	ACM723X	1942	ACM742X	1961	ACM761X
1885	XEM885W	1905	XEM905W	1924	ACM724X	1943	ACM743X	1962	ACM762X
1886	XEM886W	1906	XEM906W	1925	ACM725X	1944	ACM744X	1963	ACM763X
1887	XEM887W	1907	XEM907W	1926	ACM726X	1045	ACM745X	1964	ACM764X
1888	XCM088W	1908	XEM908W	1927	ACM727X	1946	ACM746X	1965	ACM765X
1889	XEM889W	1909	XEM909W	1928	ACM728X	1947	ACM747X	1966	ACM766X
1890	XEM890W	1910	XEM910W	1929	ACM729X	1948	ACM748X	1967	ACM767X
1891	XEM891W	1911	XEM911W	1930	ACM730X	1949	ACM749X		

Merseybus purchased many Leyland Titans from London Buses from 1992, most of which have undergone a programme of conversion to single door and refurbishment. Looking very smart in the latest livery is 2058, WYV58T pictured in Sir Thomas Street, Liverpool. *Paul Wigan*

1968-1991   Leyland Atlantean AN68D/1R   Alexander AL   H43/32F   1982

1968	ACM768X	1974	DEM774Y	1979	DEM779Y	1984	DEM784Y	1988	DEM788Y
1969	ACM769X	1975	DEM775Y	1980	DEM780Y	1985	DEM785Y	1989	DEM789Y
1970	CKB170X	1976	DEM776Y	1981	DEM781Y	1986	DEM786Y	1990	DEM790Y
1971	EKA171Y	1977	DEM777Y	1982	DEM782Y	1987	DEM787Y	1991	DEM791Y
1973	DEM773Y	1978	DEM778Y	1983	DEM783Y				

2044-2065   Leyland Titan TNLXB2RRSp   Park Royal   H44/30F   1979   Ex London Buses, 1992-94

2044	WYV44T	2046	WYV46T	2052	WYV52T	2059	WYV59T	2065	WYV65T
2045	WYV45T	2050	WYV50T	2058	WYV58T	2061	WYV61T		

2070-2220   Leyland Titan TNLXB2RRSp   Park Royal   H44/30F   1979-80   Ex London Buses, 1992-94;

2070	CUL70V	2115	CUL115V	2135	CUL135V	2161	CUL161V	2199	CUL199V
2073	CUL73V	2116	CUL116V	2136	CUL136V	2166	CUL166V	2200	CUL200V
2077	CUL77V	2117	CUL117V	2141	CUL141V	2170	CUL170V	2201	CUL201V
2082	CUL82V	2118	CUL118V	2144	CUL145V	2171	CUL171V	2203	CUL203V
2097	CUL97V	2121	CUL121V	2145	CUL145V	2174	CUL174V	2204	CUL204V
2101	CUL101V	2122	CUL122V	2147	CUL147V	2177	CUL177V	2205	CUL205V
2102	CUL102V	2123	CUL123V	2148	CUL148V	2178	CUL178V	2207	CUL207V
2103	CUL103V	2124	CUL124V	2151	CUL151V	2182	CUL182V	2210	CUL210V
2104	CUL104V	2125	CUL125V	2154	CUL154V	2184	CUL184V	2211	CUL211V
2106	CUL106V	2127	CUL127V	2155	CUL155V	2187	CUL187V	2213	CUL213V
2107	CUL107V	2128	CUL128V	2156	CUL156V	2188	CUL188V	2217	CUL217V
2108	CUL108V	2129	CUL129V	2158	CUL158V	2192	CUL192V	2218	CUL218V
2109	CUL109V	2132	CUL132V	2159	CUL159V	2194	CUL194V	2219	CUL219V
2111	CUL111V	2134	CUL134V	2160	CUL160V	2196	CUL196V	2220	CUL220V

2231-2249

		Leyland Titan TNLXB-2RRSp		Park Royal		H44/30F	1980	Ex London Buses, 1992-94

2231	EYE231V	2234	EYE234V	2241	EYE241V	2243	EYE243V	2247	EYE247V
2232	EYE232V	2239	EYE239V	2242	EYE242V	2245	EYE245V	2249	EYE249V

2253-2259

		Leyland Titan TNLXB-2RR		Leyland		H44/30F	1981	Ex London Buses, 1992-93

2253	GYE253W	2256	GYE256W	2257	GYE257W	2258	GYE258W	2259	GYE259W
2255	GYE255W								

2269-2547

		Leyland Titan TNLXB2RR		Leyland		H44/30F	1981-82	Ex London Buses, 1992-94

2269	GYE269W	2333	KYV333X	2367	KYV367X	2414	KYV414X	2463	KYV463X
2271	GYE271W	2335	JGH118X	2374	KYV374X	2416	KYV416X	2464	KYV464X
2276	GYE276W	2337	KYV337X	2376	KYV376X	2417	KYV417X	2468	KYV468X
2278	GYE278W	2338	KYV338X	2382	KYV382X	2418	KYV418X	2472	KYV472X
2284	KYN284X	2339	KYV339X	2383	KYV383X	2421	KYV421X	2483	KYV483X
2289	KYN289X	2344	KYV344X	2385	KYV385X	2424	KYV424X	2484	KYV484X
2290	KYN290X	2347	KYV347X	2389	KYV389X	2425	KYV425X	2489	KYV489X
2293	KYN293X	2350	KYV350X	2391	KYV391X	2426	KYV426X	2491	KYV491X
2299	KYN299X	2351	KYV351X	2393	KYV393X	2427	KYV427X	2494	KYV494X
2301	KYN301X	2353	KYV353X	2398	KYV398X	2430	KYV430X	2499	KYV499X
2303	KYN303X	2354	KYV354X	2400	KYV400X	2431	KYV431X	2509	KYV509X
2304	KYN304X	2355	KYV355X	2402	KYV402X	2436	KYV436X	2520	KYV520X
2315	KYN315X	2359	KYV359X	2407	KYV407X	2440	KYV440X	2528	KYV528X
2316	KYN316X	2363	KYV363X	2409	KYV409X	2443	KYV443X	2534	KYV534X
2324	KYV324X	2364	KYV364X	2412	KYV412X	2449	KYV449X	2538	KYV538X
2330	KYV330X	2365	KYV365X	2413	KYV413X	2450	KYV450X	2547	KYV547X
2332	KYV332X								

2561-2884

		Leyland Titan TNLXB2RR*		Leyland		H44/30F*	1982-84	Ex London Buses, 1992-94
								*2878/9/84 are TNTL112RR

2561	NUW561Y	2638	NUW638Y	2692	OHV692Y	2730	OHV730Y	2754	OHV754Y
2570	NUW570Y	2655	NUW655Y	2695	OHV695Y	2733	OHV733Y	2878	A878SUL
2599	NUW599Y	2656	NUW656Y	2698	OHV698Y	2741	OHV741Y	2879	A879SUL
2612	NUW612Y	2682	OHV682Y	2703	OHV703Y	2746	OHV746Y	2884	A884SUL
2628	NUW628Y	2690	OHV690Y	2726	OHV726Y	2753	OHV753Y		

3003	GBU3V	MCW Metrobus DR101/6	MCW		H43/30F	1979	Ex Stevensons, 1994
3010	GBU10V	MCW Metrobus DR101/6	MCW		H43/30F	1979	Ex Stevensons, 1993
3026	WYW26T	MCW Metrobus DR101/8	MCW		H43/28D	1979	Ex London Buses, 1993

3074-3081

		MCW Metrobus DR102/20		MCW		H46/31F	1981	Ex Newport, 1994

3074	JBO74W	3077	JBO77W	3078	JBO78W	3079	JBO79W	3081	JBO81W
3076	JBO76W								

3144	JHE144W	MCW Metrobus DR104/6	MCW		H46/31F	1981	Ex Stevensons, 1993
3152	JHE152W	MCW Metrobus DR104/6	MCW		H46/31F	1981	Ex Stevensons, 1994
3156	JHE156W	MCW Metrobus DR104/6	MCW		H46/31F	1981	Ex Stevensons, 1994

M9-M199

		MCW Metrobus DR101/9		MCW		H43/28D	1978-79	Ex London Northern, 1994

M9	WYW9T	M67	WYW67T	M92	WYW92T	M118	BYX118V	M148	BYX148T
M12	WYW12T	M72	WYW72T	M95	WYW95T	M124	BYX124V	M160	BYX160T
M25	WYW25T	M75	WYW75T	M98	BYX98V	M126	BYX126V	M161	BYX161T
M27	WYW27T	M78	WYW78T	M101	BYX101V	M130	BYX130V	M181	BYX181T
M32	WYW32T	M79	WYW79T	M103	BYX103V	M133	BYX133V	M189	BYX189T
M33	WYW33T	M80	WYW80T	M114	BYX114V	M139	BYX139V	M194	BYX194T
M35	WYW35T	M81	WYW81T	M115	BYX115V	M145	BYX145V	M199	BYX199T
M42	WYW42T	M82	WYW82T	M117	BYX117V				

North and south are represented in these colour views of members of the MTL fleet. *Opposite, top:* One of the Titans now based at Gillmoss depot is 2243, EYE243V with, interestingly, new blinds to the London-specified display . *Paul Wigan*

Opposite, bottom: This lower picture shows 1203, L203SKD in the MTL London livery which uses the MTL logo style on a red base to comply with the London Transport requirement. Olympian 1203 is one which came from Liverbus during 1995 and then worked on the London Suburban operations in north London. Similar styled buses but with single door layout are now entering service in the Wirral and at Southport. *Richard Godfrey*

Pictured passing Marble Arch is Routemaster RML2699, SMK699F. The nineteen longer Routemasters are currently allocated to Holloway for the MTL London operation. *M E Lyons*

M231-M481
MCW Metrobus DR101/12   MCW   H43/28D   1980   Ex London Northern, 1994

M231	BYX231V	M294	BYX294V	M328	EYE328V	M356	GYE356W	M481	GYE481W
M243	BYX243V	M322	EYE322V	M341	EYE341V		

M231 BYX231V   M294 BYX294V   M328 EYE328V   M356 GYE356W   M481 GYE481W
M243 BYX243V   M322 EYE322V   M341 EYE341V

3502-3509
MCW Metrobus DR101/7   MCW   H46/31F   1980   Ex Yorkshire Rider, 1995

3502 JUM502V   3504 JUM504V   3506 PUA506W   3508 PUA508W   3509 PUA510W
3503 JUM503V   3505 JUM505V   3507 JUM501V

3510-3514
MCW Metrobus DR103/4   MCW   DPH43/30F* 1980   Ex Badgerline, 1994
*3510 is DPH43/29F

3510 DAE510W   3511 DAE511W   3512 DAE512W   3513 DAE513W   3514 DAE514W

M512-M802
MCW Metrobus DR101/14   MCW   H43/28D   1980   Ex London Northern, 1994

M512 GYE512W   M571 GYE571W   M594 GYE594W   M656 KYV656X   M755 KYV755X
M560 GYE560W   M572 GYE572W   M608 KYO608X   M674 KYV674X   M764 KYV764X
M561 GYE561W   M574 GYE574W   M616 KYO616X   M677 KYV677X   M797 KYV797X
M563 GYE563W   M576 GYE576W   M620 KYO620X   M678 KYV678X   M800 KYV800X
M564 GYE564W   M578 GYE578W   M623 KYO623X   M693 KYV693X   M801 KYV801X
M565 GYE565W   M579 GYE579W   M639 KYV639X   M739 KYV739X   M802 KYV803X
M570 GYE570W   M588 GYE588W   M640 KYV640X

M804 KYV804X   MCW Metrobus DR101/14   MCW   O43/28D   1980   Ex London Northern, 1994

M824-M934
MCW Metrobus DR101/16   MCW   H43/28D   1983-84 Ex London Northern, 1994

M024 OJD824Y   M879 OJD879Y   M899 A899SUL   M916 A916SUL   M925 A925SUL
M829 OJD829Y   M890 OJD890Y   M912 A912SUL   M917 A917SUL   M928 A928SUL
M876 OJD876Y   M896 OJD896Y   M915 A915SUL   M921 A921SUL   M934 A934SUL
M878 OJD878Y

M1045 A745THV   MCW Metrobus DR101/19   MCW   DPH43/28D 1984   Ex London Northern, 1994
M1052 A752THV   MCW Metrobus DR101/19   MCW   H43/28D   1984   Ex London Northern, 1994

Where Metrobuses have been allocated main series numbers they have appeared in the 3xxx series which is where the current MTL London examples rest. Representing the type is M1067, B67WUL seen working service 82 at Victoria station. *M E Lyons*

M1058-M1163

MCW Metrobus DR101/17   MCW   H43/28D   1984-85   Ex London Northern, 1994

M1058	B58WUL	M1076	B76WUL	M1113	B113WUL	M1143	B143WUL
M1059	B59WUL	M1077	B77WUL	M1114	B114WUL	M1145	B145WUL
M1060	B60WUL	M1078	B78WUL	M1115	B115WUL	M1146	B146WUL
M1061	B61WUL	M1079	B79WUL	M1117	B117WUL	M1147	B147WUL
M1063	B63WUL	M1080	B80WUL	M1118	B118WUL	M1148	B148WUL
M1065	B65WUL	M1081	B81WUL	M1119	B119WUL	M1149	B149WUL
M1066	B66WUL	M1082	B82WUL	M1120	B120WUL	M1150	B150WUL
M1067	B67WUL	M1083	B83WUL	M1141	B141WUL	M1151	B151WUL
M1072	B72WUL	M1111	B111WUL	M1142	B142WUL		

M1153	B153WUL
M1156	B156WUL
M1157	B157WUL
M1158	B158WUL
M1159	B159WUL
M1160	B160WUL
M1161	B161WUL
M1163	B163WUL

M1234-M1414

MCW Metrobus DR101/17   MCW   H43/28D   1984-85   Ex London Northern, 1994

M1234	B234WUL	M1292	B292WUL	M1333	C333BUV	M1385	C385BUV	M1395	C395BUV
M1250	B250WUL	M1325	C325BUV	M1334	C334BUV	M1390	C390BUV	M1396	C396BUV
M1277	B277WUL	M1329	C329BUV	M1355	C355BUV	M1392	C392BUV	M1397	C397BUV
M1284	B284WUL	M1330	C330BUV	M1365	C365BUV	M1393	C393BUV	M1403	C403BUV
M1287	B287WUL	M1331	C331BUV	M1369	C369BUV	M1394	C394BUV	M1414	C414BUV

5287	BYW387V	Leyland National 10351A/2R		B44F	1979	Ex Blue Triangle, 1994
5294	BCW823V	Leyland National 2 NL106L11/1R		B44F	1980	Ex Ribble, 1995
5295	BCW824V	Leyland National 2 NL106L11/1R		B44F	1980	Ex Ribble, 1995
5296	DBV836W	Leyland National 2 NL106L11/1R		B44F	1980	Ex Ribble, 1995
5297	DBV840W	Leyland National 2 NL106L11/1R		B44F	1980	Ex Ribble, 1995
5298	LFR863X	Leyland National 2 NL106L11/1R		B44F	1981	Ex Ribble, 1995
5299	LFR872X	Leyland National 2 NL106L11/1R		B44F	1981	Ex Ribble, 1995

6035-6041

Leyland National 2 NL116L11/1R   B49F   1979-80

6035	UEM35V	6037	UEM37V	6039	UEM39V	6040	UEM40V	6041	UEM41V
6036	UEM36V	6038	UEM38V						

6059	PJI5916	Leyland National 11351A/1R		B49F	1978	
6062	HCW762N	Leyland National 11351/1R		B49F	1975	Ex Raja, Blackburn, 1993

6101-6138

Leyland National 2 NL116L11/1R   B49F   1980

6101	VBG101V	6109	VBG109V	6117	VBG117V	6125	WWM908W	6132	WWM911W
6102	VBG102V	6110	VBG110V	6118	VBG118V	6126	WWM909W	6133	VBG133V
6103	VBG103V	6111	VBG111V	6119	VBG119V	6127	VBG127V	6134	WWM912W
6104	VBG104V	6112	VBG112V	6120	VBG120V	6128	VBG128V	6135	WWM913W
6105	VBG105V	6113	VBG113V	6121	VBG121V	6129	VBG129V	6136	WWM914W
6106	VBG106V	6114	VBG114V	6122	VBG122V	6130	VBG130V	6137	WWM915W
6107	VBG107V	6115	VBG115V	6124	WWM907W	6131	WWM910W	6138	WWM916W
6108	VBG108V	6116	VBG116V						

6139-6172

Leyland National 2 NL116AL11/1R   B49F*   1981-82   *6147-51 are B23DL

6139	XLV139W	6145	XLV145W	6151	XLV151W	6157	XLV157W	6168	CKB165X
6140	XLV140W	6146	XLV146W	6152	XLV152W	6158	XLV158W	6169	CKB166X
6141	XLV141W	6147	XLV147W	6153	XLV153W	6159	XLV159W	6170	CKB167X
6142	XLV142W	6148	XLV148W	6154	XLV154W	6160	XLV160W	6171	CKB168X
6143	XLV143W	6149	XLV149W	6155	XLV155W	6161	XLV161W	6172	CKB169X
6144	XLV144W	6150	XLV150W	6156	XLV156W	6162	XLV162W		

6177	RSG817V	Leyland National 2 NL116L11/1R(6HLXB)		B52F	1980	Ex Fife Scottish, 1993
6196	PJI5913	Leyland National 11351A/1R		B49F	1978	
6199	BHY999V	Leyland National 2 NL106L11/1R		B41F	1980	Ex Blue Triangle, 1994
6201	KHH374W	Leyland National 2 NL116L11/1R		B52F	1980	Ex Ribble, 1995
6202	NHH379W	Leyland National 2 NL116AL11/1R		B52F	1981	Ex Ribble, 1995
6203	NHH381W	Leyland National 2 NL116AL11/1R		B52F	1981	Ex Ribble, 1995
6204	CEO723W	Leyland National 2 NL116L11/1R		B49F	1980	Ex Ribble, 1995
6205	ARN891Y	Leyland National 2 NL116HLXB/1R		B52F	1983	Ex Ribble, 1995
6206	ARN893Y	Leyland National 2 NL116HLXB/1R		B52F	1983	Ex Ribble, 1995
6207	ARN894Y	Leyland National 2 NL116HLXB/1R		B52F	1983	Ex Ribble, 1995
6211	LUA311V	Leyland National 2 NL106L11/1R		B41F	1980	Ex Blue Triangle, 1994
6301	L301TEM	Volvo B10B	Alexander Strider	B49F	1994	
6302	L302TEM	Volvo B10B	Alexander Strider	B49F	1994	
6303	L303TEM	Volvo B10B	Alexander Strider	B49F	1994	

6330-6334

DAF SB220LC550   Ikarus CitiBus   B48F   1993

6330	K130TCP	6331	K131TCP	6332	K132TCP	6333	K133TCP	6334	K510RJX

6402-6413

Aüwaerter Neoplan N4016   B33F   1993-94

6402	L402TKB	6405	L405TKB	6408	L408TKB	6410	L410TKB	6412	L412UFY
6403	L403TKB	6406	L406TKB	6409	L409TKB	6411	L411UFY	6413	L413TKB
6404	L404TKB	6407	L407TKB						

Liverbus operated thirteen Northern Counties-bodied Volvo B10Bs and these are now numbered from 6901. Seen in Liverpool with its former number is 6909, M109XKC.
Malc McDonald

Merseybus have added route-branding lettering to several of the Volvo B10Bs as shown here by 6566, M566YEW lettered for the 10A while the vehicle's blinds display 10C at the front and 10D at the side. *Paul Wigan*

6501-6543

Volvo B10B-58 — Wright Endurance — DP49F — 1994

6501	L501TKA	6510	L510TKA	6519	M519WHF	6528	M528WHF	6536	M536WHF
6502	L502TKA	6511	L511TKA	6520	M520WHF	6529	M529WHF	6537	M537WHF
6503	L503TKA	6512	L512TKA	6521	M521WHF	6530	M530WHF	6538	M538WHF
6504	L504TKA	6513	L513TKA	6522	M522WHF	6531	M531WHF	6539	M539WHF
6505	L505TKA	6514	M514WHF	6523	M523WHF	6532	M532WHF	6540	M540WHF
6506	L506TKA	6515	M515WHF	6524	M524WHF	6533	M533WHF	6541	M541WHF
6507	L507TKA	6516	M516WHF	6525	M525WHF	6534	M534WHF	6542	M542WHF
6508	L508TKA	6517	M517WHF	6526	M526WHF	6535	M535WHF	6543	M543WHF
6509	L509TKA	6518	M518WHF	6527	M527WHF				

6544-6626

Volvo B10B-58 — Wright Endurance — DP49F — 1994-96

6544	M544WTJ	6562	M562WTJ	6578	N578YEM	6594	N594CKA	6611	N611CKA
6545	M545WTJ	6563	M563WTJ	6579	N579YEM	6595	N595CKA	6612	N612CKA
6546	M546WTJ	6564	M564YEM	6570	N580YEM	6596	N596CKA	6613	N613CKA
6547	M547WTJ	6565	M565YEM	6581	N581YEM	6597	N597CKA	6614	N614CKA
6548	M548WTJ	6566	M566YEM	6582	N582YEM	6598	N598CKA	6615	N615CKA
6549	M549WTJ	6567	M567YEM	6583	N583YEM	6599	N599CKA	6616	N616CKA
6550	M550WTJ	6568	M568YEM	6584	N584CKA	6601	N601CKA	6617	N617CKA
6551	M551WTJ	6569	M569YEM	6585	N585CKA	6602	N602CKA	6618	N618CKA
6552	M552WTJ	6570	M570YEM	6586	N586CKA	6603	N603CKA	6619	N619CKA
6553	M553WTJ	6571	M571YEM	6587	N587CKA	6604	N604CKA	6620	N620CKA
6554	M554WTJ	6572	M572YEM	6588	N588CKA	6605	N605CKA	6621	N621CKA
6556	M556WTJ	6573	M573YEM	6589	N589CKA	6606	N606CKA	6622	N622CKA
6557	M557WTJ	6574	M574YEM	6590	N590CKA	6607	N607CKA	6623	N623CKA
6558	M558WTJ	6575	M575YEM	6591	N591CKA	6608	N608CKA	6624	N624CKA
6559	M559WTJ	6576	N576CKA	6592	N592CKA	6609	N609CKA	6625	N625CKA
6561	M561WTJ	6577	N577CKA	6593	N593CKA	6610	N610CKA	6626	N626CKA

A dozen Aüwaerter Neoplan N4016s were added to the Liverpool operation from 1993 for use on the City Circle, painted in Merseytravel livery with Smart names. This low-floor integral design is now a common sight in other parts of Europe, especially in Germany, though thought rather expensive in Great Britain. Shown at the side of Lime Street rail station is 6404, L404TKB. *Paul Wigan*

6901-6913

				Volvo B10B-58			Northern Counties Paladin	B51F	1993-95	Ex Liverbus, 1995

6901	K101OHF	6904	K104OHF	6907	K107OHF	6909	M109XKC	6912	M112XKC
6902	K102OHF	6905	K105OHF	6908	K108OHF	6910	M110XKC	6913	M113XKC
6903	K103OHF	6906	K106OHF						

6927	GSG127T	Leyland Leopard PSU3E/4R	Duple Dominant I	C49F	1978	Ex Fife Scottish, 1993
6930	GSG130T	Leyland Leopard PSU3E/4R	Duple Dominant I	C49F	1978	Ex Fife Scottish, 1993

7009-7020

				Leyland Tiger TRCTL11/2R			Duple Dominant IV Express	C49F	1982

7009	CKC623X	7012	CKC626X	7015	EKA215Y	7019	EKA219Y	7020	EKA220Y
7010	VKB708	7013	CKC624X	7017	EKA217Y				

VH 1	804DYE	Volvo B10M-60	Van Hool Alizée	C49FT	1988	Ex Silver Knight, Chippenham, 1995
VH 2	NJI9479	DAF MB230	Van Hool Alizée	C49FT	1989	Ex Ellison, St Helens, 1995
VH 3	G260EHD	DAF MB230LT615	Van Hool Alizée	C49FT	1989	Ex MacPhail, Motherwell, 1995
VH 4	HIL6975	Volvo B10M-61	Van Hool Alizée	C49FT	1986	Ex Movers, Boston, 1995
7031	OIW5804	Leyland Tiger TRCTL11/3R	Duple Laser	C49F	1982	Ex Duple demonstrator, 1983
7032	F32ALV	Dennis Javelin 12SDA1907	Duple 320	C50FT	1989	
7033	IIL2503	Dennis Javelin 12SDA1907	Duple 320	C50FT	1989	
7034	J34MKB	Volvo B10M-60	Plaxton Excalibur	C49FT	1992	
7035	J35MKB	Volvo B10M-60	Plaxton Excalibur	C49FT	1992	
7037	HIL5697	Volvo B10M-60	Van Hool Alizée	C49FT	1994	Ex Lee, Langley Moor, 1994
7038	HIL5698	Volvo B10M-60	Van Hool Alizée	C49FT	1994	Ex Lee, Langley Moor, 1994
7039	J531JNH	Volvo B10M-60	Jonckheere Deauville P599	C51FT	1992	Ex Liverbus, 1995
7040	A105HNC	Leyland Tiger TRCTL11/3R	Plaxton Paramount 3200	C46FT	1984	Ex Liverbus, 1995
7041	N41BWM	Volvo B10M-62	Plaxton Premiére 350	C49FT	1995	
7042	N42BWM	Volvo B10M-62	Plaxton Premiére 350	C49FT	1995	

Page 57, top: **MTL have taken a significant step forward with the intake of new single-deck buses. While several entered service in the Manchester area the current delivery will see over 100 Wright Endurance-bodied Volvo B10Bs in service. These are allocated to most operations around Liverpool. Seen here is one of the earlier batch, 6517, M517WHF allocated to Green Lane.** *Richard Godfrey*
Page 57, bottom: **The Heysham Travel fleet carries a white, yellow and green livery, the operation now using eight Leyland National 2s as well as minibuses and double-deckers. Pictured in Lancaster bus station is 6206, ARN893Y an example previously with Ribble.** *Paul Wigan*

To fulfill a need for midi-size buses the Volvo B6 has been introduced to the fleet, a batch of fifty entering service in 1994. The first, numerically, are based at Southport and carry the borough crest with 7209, L209TKA being seen on Lord Street. This vehicle has, however, since moved to St Helens.
Malc McDonald

7201-7250   Volvo B6-9.9M   Plaxton Pointer   B38F   1994

7201	L201TKA	7211	L211TKA	7221	L221TKA	7231	L231TKA	7241	L241TKA
7202	L202TKA	7212	L212TKA	7222	L222TKA	7232	L232TKA	7242	L242TKA
7203	L203TKA	7213	L213TKA	7223	L223TKA	7233	L233TKA	7243	L243TKA
7204	L204TKA	7214	L214TKA	7224	L224TKA	7234	L234TKA	7244	L244TKA
7205	L205TKA	7215	L215TKA	7225	L225TKA	7235	L235TKA	7245	L245TKA
7206	L206TKA	7216	L216TKA	7226	L226TKA	7236	L236TKA	7246	L246TKA
7207	L207TKA	7217	L217TKA	7227	L227TKA	7237	L237TKA	7247	L247TKA
7208	L208TKA	7218	L218TKA	7228	L228TKA	7238	L238TKA	7248	L248TKA
7209	L209TKA	7219	L219TKA	7229	L229TKA	7239	L239TKA	7249	L249TKA
7210	L210TKA	7220	L220TKA	7230	L230TKA	7240	L240TKA	7250	L250TKA

7301	M301YBG	Aüwaerter Neoplan N4009		B17F	1995	
7302	M302YBG	Aüwaerter Neoplan N4009		B17F	1995	
7303	M303YBG	Aüwaerter Neoplan N4009		B17F	1995	
7411	K911OEM	Dennis Dart 9.8SDL3017	Plaxton Pointer	B38F	1993	Ex Blue Triangle, 1994
7455	K955PBG	Dennis Dart 9.8SDL3017	Plaxton Pointer	B36F	1993	Ex Blue Triangle, 1994
7520	M20GGY	Dennis Dart 9.8SDL3040	Plaxton Pointer	B40F	1994	Ex Ogdens, Haydock, 1995
7530	M30GGY	Dennis Dart 9.8SDL3040	Plaxton Pointer	B40F	1994	Ex Ogdens, Haydock, 1995

7679-7691   Renault-Dodge S56   Alexander AM   B23F   1986-87

7679	D679SEM	7683	D683SEM	7685	D685SEM	7688	D688SEM	7690	D690SEM
7680	D680SEM	7684	D684SEM	7687	D687SEM	7689	D689SEM	7691	D691SEM
7682	D682SEM								

7753	C553BHY	Ford Transit 190	Dormobile	B16F	1986	Ex Woodhead, Morecambe, 1993
7754	C54WBF	Ford Transit 190	Dormobile	B16F	1986	Ex Watson, Lancaster, 1993
7767	D229GLJ	Freight Rover Sherpa	Dormobile	B16F	1986	Ex Bolton Coachways, 1994
7768	D412FEH	Freight Rover Sherpa	PMT Bursley	B16F	1986	Ex Bolton Coachways, 1994
7769	D130NON	Freight Rover Sherpa	Dormobile	B16F	1986	Ex Bolton Coachways, 1994

Three examples of the seventeen-seater Aüwaerter Neoplan N4009 are used by MTL for the Merseyrider operation though they currently carry Merseytravel's yellow livery. Seen in Newton-le-Willows is 7301, M301YBG. *Roy Marshall*

7801-7810

Optare MetroRider | Optare | B22F* | 1994 | *7802/3 are B17F

| 7801 | K801NTJ | 7803 | K803NTJ | 7805 | K805NTJ | 7807 | L807TFY | 7809 | L809TFY |
| 7802 | K802NTJ | 7804 | K804NTJ | 7806 | K806NTJ | 7808 | L808TFY | 7810 | L810TFY |

| 7811 | N811CKA | Optare MetroRider | Optare | B22F | 1995 |

7817-DRL37

Dennis Dart 9SDL3016 | Plaxton Pointer | B34F | 1992 | Ex London Northern, 1994

7817	K817NKH	SRL22	K822NKH	DRL26	K826NKH	DRL30	K830OKH	DRL34	K834OKH
DRL18	K818NKH	DRL23	K823NKH	DRL27	K827NKH	DRL31	K831OKH	DRL35	K835OKH
DRL19	K819NKH	DRL24	K824NKH	DRL28	K828NKH	DRL32	K832OKH	DRL36	K836OKH
DRL20	K820NKH	DRL25	K825NKH	DRL29	K829OKH	DRL33	K833OKH	DRL37	K837OKH
DRL21	K821NKH								

M210-M222

Optare MetroRider MR03 | Optare | B26F | 1991 | Ex London Northern, 1994

M210	J210BWU	M213	J213BWU	M216	J216BWU	M218	J218BWU	M220	J220BWU
M211	J211BWU	M214	J214BWU	M217	J217BWU	M219	J219BWU	M221	J221BWU
M212	J212BWU	M215	J215BWU						

7918-7937

Mercedes-Benz 811D | Wright NimBus | B26F | 1993 | Ex London Northern, 1994

MW18	NDZ7918	MW22	NDZ7922	MW26	NDZ7926	MW30	NDZ7930	MW34	NDZ7934
MW19	NDZ7919	MW23	NDZ7923	MW27	NDZ7927	MW31	NDZ7931	MW35	NDZ7935
MW20	NDZ7920	MW24	NDZ7924	MW28	NDZ7928	MW32	NDZ7932	MW36	K510FYN
MW21	NDZ7921	MW25	NDZ7925	MW29	NDZ7929	MW33	NDZ7933	MW37	K476FYN

7941	G801OVA	Mercedes-Benz 811D	Optare StarRider	B27F	1990	Ex Viscount, 1992
7942	G802OVA	Mercedes-Benz 811D	Optare StarRider	B27F	1990	Ex Viscount, 1992
7943	G803OVA	Mercedes-Benz 811D	Oplare StarRider	B27F	1990	Ex Viscount, 1993
7944	G804OVA	Mercedes-Benz 811D	Optare StarRider	B27F	1990	Ex Viscount, 1993

7945-7949 — Mercedes-Benz 811D — Marshall — B27F — 1993

| 7945 | K945OEM | 7946 | K946OEM | 7947 | K947OEM | 7948 | K948OEM | 7949 | K949OEM |

7950	G950RFL	Mercedes-Benz 811D	Carlyle	B31F	1990	Ex Cambus, 1993
7951	G951RFL	Mercedes-Benz 811D	Carlyle	B31F	1990	Ex Cambus, 1993
7952	G952RFL	Mercedes-Benz 811D	Carlyle	B31F	1990	Ex Cambus, 1993
7953	G953RFL	Mercedes-Benz 811D	Carlyle	B31F	1990	Ex Cambus, 1993

SR108-SR121 — Mercedes-Benz 811D — Optare StarRider — B26F — 1989 — London Northern, 1994

SR108	G108KUB	SR111	G111KUB	SR114	G114KUB	SR117	G117KUB	SR120	G120KUB
SR109	G109KUB	SR112	G112KUB	SR115	G115KUB	SR118	G118KUB	SR121	G121KUB
SR110	G110KUB	SR113	G113KUB	SR116	G116KUB				

DNL101-120 — Dennis Dart 9SDL3034 — Northern Counties — B34F — 1994 — Ex London Buses, 1994

101	L101HHV	105	L105HHV	109	L109HHV	114	L114HHV	118	L118HHV
102	L102HHV	106	L106HHV	110	L110HHV	115	L115HHV	119	L119HHV
103	L103HHV	107	L107HHV	112	L112HHV	116	L116HHV	120	L120HHV
104	L104HHV	108	L108HHV	113	L113HHV	117	L117HHV		

RM29-RM2186 — AEC Routemaster 5RM — Park Royal — H36/28R — 1959-65 — Ex London Northern, 1994

RM 29	OYM453A	RM1158	158CLT	RM1287	287CLT	RM1799	799DYE	RM2023	ALM23B
RM268	VLT268	RM1171	171CLT	RM1348	348CLT	RM1804	EYY327B	RM2041	ALM41B
RM446	WLT446	RM1185	XYJ427	RM1568	568CLT	RM1840	840DYE	RM2136	CUV136C
RM646	KFF257	RM1218	218CLT	RM1700	KGJ167A	RM1971	ALM971B	RM2153	CUV153C
RM765	WLT765	RM1283	283CLT	RM1758	758DYE	RM1979	ALM979B	RM2186	CUV186C
RM912	WLT912								

RML903 WTL903 — AEC Routemaster 7RM — Park Royal — H40/32R — 1961 — Ex London Northern, 1994

RML2282-2731 — AEC Routemaster 7RM — Park Royal — H40/32R — 1965-67 — Ex London Northern, 1994

2282	CUV282C	2310	CUV310C	2413	JJD413D	2561	JJD561D	2679	SMK679F
2284	CUV284C	2367	JJD367D	2419	JJD419D	2603	NML603E	2699	SMK699F
2295	CUV295C	2393	JJD393D	2479	JJD479D	2620	NML620E	2731	SMK731F
2296	CUV296C	2395	JJD395D	2511	JJD511D				

R&I *(Currently in a separate numbering sequence)*

058	E783MLB	Iveco 35.8	Devon Conversions	M8	1988	Ex R & I, 1995
067	ULL897	Mercedes-Benz 811D	Optare StarRider	DP29F	1988	Ex R & I, 1995
077	C945FMJ	Ford Transit 190	Chassis Developments	M8	1985	Ex R & I, 1995
081	RIB6197	Kässbohrer Setra S210HI	Kässbohrer Optimal	C26FT	1989	Ex R & I, 1995
082	RIB6198	Kässbohrer Setra S210HI	Kässbohrer Optimal	C26FT	1989	Ex R & I, 1995
083	RIB6199	Kässbohrer Setra S210HI	Kässbohrer Optimal	C26FT	1989	Ex R & I, 1995
087	F87GGC	Mercedes-Benz 811D	Robin Hood	DP29F	1989	Ex R & I, 1995
090	F90GGC	Mercedes-Benz 811D	Robin Hood	DP29F	1989	Ex R & I, 1995
091	RIB8432	Iveco Daily 49.10	Robin Hood City Nippy	DP12F	1989	Ex R & I, 1995
092	WPX448	Toyota Coaster HB31R	Caetano Optimo	C18F	1990	Ex R & I, 1995
093	165BXP	Mercedes-Benz 811D	Optare StarRider	C29F	1992	Ex R & I, 1995
094	672DYA	Toyota Coaster HDB30R	Caetano Optimo II	C21F	1991	Ex R & I, 1995
202	RIB5082	Iveco Daily 49.10	Robin Hood City Nippy	B23F	1989	Ex R & I, 1995
203	RIB5083	Iveco Daily 49.10	Robin Hood City Nippy	B23F	1989	Ex R & I, 1995
206	RIB4316	Iveco Daily 49.10	Robin Hood City Nippy	B15F	1989	Ex R & I, 1995
207	RIB7003	Iveco Daily 49.10	Robin Hood City Nippy	B23F	1989	Ex R & I, 1995
208	RIB7004	Iveco Daily 49.10	LHE	B23F	1990	Ex R & I, 1995
210	G122CLD	Iveco Daily 49.10	Robin Hood City Nippy	B19F	1989	Ex R & I, 1995

216-226 — Dennis Dart 9SDL3002 — Carlyle Dartline — B36F — 1990 — Ex R & I, 1995

| 216 | G216LGK | 220 | G220LGK | 224 | G124RGT | 229 | G129RGT | 232 | RIB7002 |
| 219 | G219LGK | 221 | G121RGT | | | | | | |

233 33LUG — Dennis Dart 9.8SDL3017 — Plaxton Pointer — B40F — 1002 — Ex H & I, 1995

234-241 — Dennis Dart 9SDL3011 — Plaxton Pointer — B35F — 1993-94 — Ex R & I, 1995

| 234 | K414MGN | 236 | K416MGN | 238 | K418MGN | 240 | M498ALP | 241 | M499ALP |
| 235 | RIB5085 | 237 | K417MGN | 239 | K419MGN | | | | |

The R & I Buses livery is being replaced by the all-red MTL London scheme. Pictured outside the Brent Cross shopping centre while working London Transport service 112 is 249, M507ALP, an Optare Vecta product which is based on the MAN 11.190 chassis. *Richard Godfrey*

242	RIB8431	Dennis Dart 9.8SDL30..	Marshall C37	B40F	1994	Ex R & I, 1995
243	M501ALP	Optare MetroRider	Optare	B25F	1995	Ex R & I, 1995
244	M502ALP	Optare MetroRider	Optare	B25F	1995	Ex R & I, 1995
245	M503ALP	Dennis Dart 9.8SDL3017	Plaxton Pointer	B40F	1995	Ex R & I, 1995
246	M504ALP	Dennis Dart 9.8SDL3017	Plaxton Pointer	B40F	1995	Ex R & I, 1995
247	M505ALP	Dennis Dart 9.8SDL3017	Plaxton Pointer	B40F	1995	Ex R & I, 1995
248	M506ALP	Dennis Dart 9.8SDL3017	Plaxton Pointer	B40F	1995	Ex R & I, 1995

249-253		MAN 11.190		Optare Vecta		B42F	1995

249	M507ALP	**250**	M508ALP	**251**	N701FLN	**252**	N702FLN	**253**	N703FLN

303	D85DOT	Mercedes-Benz 609D	Robin Hood	DP14F	1987	Ex R & I, 1995
330	SVO89	Volvo B10M-60	Plaxton Paramount 3500 III	C49FT	1990	Ex R & I, 1995
333	43FJF	Volvo B10M-60	Plaxton Paramount 3500 III	C49FT	1990	Ex R & I, 1995
334	RIB5084	Volvo B10M-60	Plaxton Paramount 3500 III	C53F	1990	Ex R & I, 1995
336	RIB5086	Volvo B10M-60	Plaxton Paramount 3500 III	C49FT	1990	Ex R & I, 1995
337	RIB7017	Volvo B10M-60	Plaxton Paramount 3500 III	C49FT	1990	Ex R & I, 1995
338	RIB7018	Volvo B10M-60	Plaxton Paramount 3500 III	C49FT	1990	Ex R & I, 1995
341	OO1942	Volvo B10M-60	Plaxton Paramount 3500 III	C49FT	1991	Ex R & I, 1995
342	RIB4315	LAG G355Z	LAG Panoramic	C36FT	1989	Ex R & I, 1995
343	N713FLN	Iveco 59.12	Cacciamalli	C20F	1995	Ex R & I, 1995
344	N714FLN	Iveco 59.12	Cacciamalli	C20F	1995	Ex R & I, 1995
345	N715FLN	Mercedes-Benz 814D	Cacciamalli	C20F	1995	
346	N716FLN	Mercedes-Benz 814D	Cacciamalli	C20F	1995	Ex R & I, 1995
347	N717FLN	Mercedes-Benz 814D	Cacciamalli	C20F	1995	Ex R & I, 1995
348	N698FLN	Iveco 40.10	Robin Hood	C12F	1995	
539	H539YCX	DAF SB220LC550	Ikarus Citi Bus	B50F	1991	Ex Ogden's, St Helens, 1995
848	F848YJX	DAF SB220LC550	Optare Delta	B49F	1989	Ex Ogden's, St Helens, 1995
849	F849YJX	DAF SB220LC550	Optare Delta	DP48F	1989	Ex Ogden's, St Helens, 1995
901	RIB6195	Kässbohrer Setra S215HR	Kässbohrer Rational	C49FT	1987	Ex R & I, 1995

Operations:

Wirral: 0064-8, 0201-10/2/51/65-87, 1041/8/67-70, 1473/80/2/6/8-92, 1507/11/3/5/7/8/87-90/5/7, 1626-8/31/2/4-7/9/42/4/6, 1873-80/8-900, 1902-7/21-30/43-50/63-5, 6330-4, 7235-42, 7301, 7679/8/2-5/91, 7801-6.
St Helens: 0252-60, 0801-28, 2289/99/301/3/4/15/6/24/32/3/7/8/50/3-5/63/5/98, 2400/9/43/68, 6035-8/40, 6101-4/11-16/21/2/39/40/7/8/52-62/8-72, 6204, 6501-13, 7209-14/6/8/28-30/2, 7520/30, 7941-3
Southport: 0261-4, 1035/6, 1449, 1524/51, 1612, 1976-87, 6106-10/24-38, 6514-6/24/7/8/44-6/58/9, 7201-8/17.
Sightseers: 0001/2/20-3/30/4/40/1, 0193/4, 0507, 1300, 1847, 6149/50, 7009/10/3/5/7/9/31-5/7-42/61-3, 3507/8/14
Merseyrider: 1042-7/9-63, 1700/3/5/6/13-5/20/4/6-8, 6151, 7302/3, 7215/20-2/31/3/4/46-50, 7411/55, 7817, 7948-53
Fareway: 0093-7/9, 0159-68/72-5, 0213-5, 0369/74-7/9/81/4/92/3/6/8, 0701-10/21, 2416/7/27/30, 3074/6-9, 3502-4/9, 6547-57, 7243-5, 78-7-11, 7944-7.
Liverbus: 0361/2, 1125/6/8/31/2/4-6/9/43/4/6/8, 1211/8/9, 5294-9, 6039/41/105/17-21, 6901-10/2/3.
MTL Heysham: 0042/3/57-60, 3003/10, 3505, 6177/99, 6201-3/5-7, 6927, 7012/20, 7753/67-70.
R&I: As supplement plus VH1-4 & DRL30/5/6.
London: Those still with London buses numbers less VH1-4 & DRL30/5/6, plus 539, 848/9.
Merseybus: remainder

Livery and operations: Cream and crimson (Merseybus, MTL Lancashire, Southport and District, Sightseers); yellow, white and black (Merseytravel/Smart); green and yellow (MTL Heysham); red (MTL London); green and cream (Merseyrider); silver and maroon (Silver Service).

Previous registrations:

165BXP	J361BNW	KGJ167A	700DYE	RIB5086	G86RGG
33LUG	J823GGF	L411UFY	L175THF	RIB6195	D396DPE
43RJF	G43RGG	L412UFY	L176THF	RIB6197	F81GGC
804DYE	F967GMW	MCN30K	NNL49	RIB6198	F82GGC
ACM768X	DKF683X	NJI9479	D276XCX	RIB6199	F83GGC
ACM769X	DKF684X	OIW5804	BCK314Y	RIB7002	CMN12A, H403HOY
CKB170X	DKF685X	OO1942	H608UWR	RIB7003	F207HGN
EYY327B	804DYE	OYM453A	VLT29	RIB7004	G208LGK
G122CLD	G210LGK, RIB5086	PJI5913	RKA874T	RIB7017	G77RGG
HIL5697	D637MSJ	PJI5916	RKA867T	RIB7018	G78RGG
HIL5698	D638MSJ	RIB4315	F504YNV, A17AML	RIB8431	L416PAR
HIL6975	C29VJF	RIB4316	F206HGN	RIB8432	F91JGJ
IIL2503	F33ALV	RIB5082	F202HGN	SOV89	G44RGG
JGH118X	KYV335X, 324CLT	RIB5083	F203HGN	ULL897	E200UWT
K476FYN	NDZ7937	RIB5084	G74RGG	VKB708	CKC625X
K510FYN	NDZ7936	RIB5085	K415MGN	XYJ427	F967GMW
KFF257	WLT646				

The index marks for MTL London's Mercedes-Benz fleet neatly fall into the main numbering scheme, though only time will tell if these will be confirmed. Seen at Brent Cross is MW28, NDZ7928, one of the batch with Wright NimBus bodywork.
Richard Godfrey

NIP-ON

K G Hatton, 26 Haywood Gardens, West Park, St Helens, Merseyside, WA10 4JU

Depots: Shaw Street, St Helens

	Reg	Chassis	Body	Seating	Year	History
	MNY892X	Leyland Leopard PSU3A/4R	Duple Dominant II(1983)	C53F	1970	Ex Parfitt's, 1995
	BFV900R	Leyland Leopard PSU4D/2R	Duple Dominant	B47F	1977	Ex South Lancs, St Helens, 1995
	PTD672S	Leyland National 11351A/1R		B49F	1978	Ex Bridge, Gourock, 1992
	LUA330V	Leyland National 2 NL106L11/1R		B41F	1980	Ex Victoria Travel, Earlestown, 1994
	YSX931W	Leyland National 2 NL106L11/1R		B41F	1981	Ex Victoria Travel, Earlestown, 1994
	NPA226W	Leyland Leopard PSU3E/4R	Plaxton Supreme IV Express	C53F	1981	Ex South Lancs, St Helens, 1996
	NPA227W	Leyland Leopard PSU3E/4R	Plaxton Supreme IV Express	C53F	1981	Ex Victoria Travel, Earlestown, 1994
	NPA232W	Leyland Leopard PSU3E/4R	Plaxton Supreme IV Express	C53F	1981	Ex Victoria Travel, Earlestown, 1994
	UWY63X	Leyland Leopard PSU3F/2R	Duple Dominant IV Express	C49F	1981	Ex South Lancs, St Helens, 1996
	HSB739Y	Volvo B10M-61	Duple Goldliner IV	C53F	1983	Ex Victoria Travel, Earlestown, 1995
	HSB740Y	Volvo B10M-61	Duple Goldliner IV	C53F	1983	Ex Victoria Travel, Earlestown, 1995
	A304JFA	Leyland National 2 NL116HLXCT/1R		DP47F	1984	Ex PMT, 1992
	A305JFA	Leyland National 2 NL116HLXCT/1R		DP47F	1984	Ex PMT, 1993
	A306JFA	Leyland National 2 NL116HLXCT/1R		DP47F	1984	Ex PMT, 1993
w	D804MNY	Renault-Dodge S56	East Lancashire	DP22F	1987	Ex Heaton Travel, Leigh, 1994
	D868MDB	Renault-Dodge S56	Northern Counties	B20F	1987	Ex Clydeside 2000, 1994
	D893DSF	Renault-Dodge S56	Alexander AM	B25F	1987	Ex Fife Scottish, 1994

Previous Registrations:

BFV900R	PHB364R, PJI9172	HSB740Y	TSD149Y, WLT774
HSB739Y	TSD148Y, WLT538	MNY892X	WHA243H

Livery: Blue and red

Nip-on currently operate three of the six Gardner-engined dual-purpose Leyland National 2s new to PMT. Pictured in St Helens is A306JFA which still retains the high-back seating. *Paul Wigan*

NORTH WESTERN

North Western Road Car Co Ltd, Liverline Travel Services Ltd,
73 Ormskirk Road, Aintree, Liverpool, Merseyside, L9 5AE
The Bee Line Buzz Company, Hulme Hall Road, Manchester, M15 4LY
Arrowline (Travel) Ltd, PO Box 32, Knutsford, Cheshire, WA16 6BD

A subsidiary of British Bus plc
Depots and outstations: Hawthorne Road, Bootle; Stanley Road, Knutsford; Holden Road, Leigh; Hulme Hall Road, Manchester; Beechwood, Runcorn; Neverstitch Road, Skelmersdale, Athlone Road, Warrington; Wallgate, Wigan; Road Four, Winsford Industrial Estate, Winsford and Wythenshaw.

| 1 | E224BVR | Renault-Dodge S46 | Northern Counties | B24F | 1988 | Ex Little White Buses, 1995 |
| 2 | E225BVR | Renault-Dodge S46 | Northern Counties | B24F | 1988 | Ex Little White Buses, 1995 |

3-35

| | | Renault-Dodge S46 | Northern Counties | B22F | 1987 | Ex Ribble, 1989 |

3	D403NNA	9	D409NNA	17	D417NNA	24	D424NNA	28	D428NNA
4	D404NNA	10	D410NNA	18	D418NNA	25	D425NNA	31	D431NNA
5	D405NNA	11	D411NNA	19	D419NNA	26	D426NNA	33	D433NNA
6	D406NNA	13	D413NNA	21	D421NNA	27	D427NNA	35	D435NNA
8	D408NNA	16	D416NNA						

36	E386CNE	Renault-Dodge S56	Northern Counties	B23F	1988	Ex Little White Buses, 1995
37	D437NNA	Renault-Dodge S56	Northern Counties	B22F	1987	Ex Ribble, 1989
39	D439NNA	Renault-Dodge S56	Northern Counties	B22F	1987	Ex Ribble, 1989
42	D442NNA	Renault-Dodge S56	Northern Counties	B22F	1987	Ex Ribble, 1989
44	J644LKD	Renault-Dodge S56	Northern Counties	B22F	1991	Ex Little White Buses, 1995
45	D445NNA	Renault-Dodge S56	Northern Counties	B22F	1987	Ex Ribble, 1989
46	D446NNA	Renault-Dodge S56	Northern Counties	B22F	1987	Ex Ribble, 1989
50	J78MHF	Mercedes-Benz 709D	Wright	B29F	1992	Ex Amberline, 1993
51	J734MFY	Mercedes-Benz 709D	Wright	B29F	1992	Ex Amberline, 1993
52	J735MFY	Mercedes-Benz 709D	Wright	B29F	1992	Ex Amberline, 1993

53-67

| | | Mercedes-Benz 709D | Alexander Sprint | B25F | 1994 |

53	L153UEM	56	L156UEM	59	M59WKA	62	M62WKA	65	M65WKA
54	L154UEM	57	M157WWM	60	M160WTJ	63	M63WKA	66	M166WTJ
55	L155UEM	58	M158WWM	61	M61WKA	64	M64WKA	67	M67WKA

| 68 | H407BVR | Mercedes-Benz 609D | Reeve Burgess Beaver | B20F | 1990 | Ex Star Line, 1995 |
| 69 | L647DNA | Mercedes-Benz 709D | Marshall C19 | B29F | 1994 | Ex Star Line, 1995 |

Ten Dennis Lance with Plaxton Verde bodywork entered service with North Western during 1995 in all-white livery. Pictured in Liverpool on the X5 service is 1202, M202YKA which arrives vinyl patches for City Express services such as the X5 on which it is seen operating.
Paul Wigan

70-95 — Mercedes-Benz 811D — Carlyle — B33F — 1989-90

70	G100TND	75	G105TND	78	G108TND	82	G112TND	93	G123TJA
72	G102TND	76	G106TND	79	G109TND	88	G118TND	94	G124TJA
73	G103TND	77	G107TND	80	G110TND	89	G119TND	95	G125TJA
74	G104TND								

96	J291NNB	Mercedes-Benz 709D	Carlyle	B29F	1991	Ex Star Line, 1995
97	J292NNB	Mercedes-Benz 709D	Carlyle	B29F	1991	Ex Star Line, 1995
98	J293NNB	Mercedes-Benz 709D	Carlyle	B29F	1991	Ex Star Line, 1995
99	H129CDB	Mercedes-Benz 811D	LHE Commuter	B31F	1990	Ex C-Line, 1993
100	H130CDB	Mercedes-Benz 811D	LHE Commuter	B31F	1990	Ex C-Line, 1992

101-105 — Mercedes-Benz 709D — Alexander Sprint — DP23F — 1994

101	M101WKA	102	M102WKA	103	M103WKA	104	M104WKA	105	M105WKA

106	K880UDB	Mercedes-Benz 814D	Dormobile Routemaker	DP29F	1993	Ex Star Line, 1995
107	L646DNA	Mercedes-Benz 709D	Dormobile Routemaker	B29F	1994	Ex Star Line, 1995
108	L648DNA	Mercedes-Benz 709D	Marshall C19	B29F	1994	Ex Star Line, 1995
109	L649DNA	Mercedes-Benz 709D	Marshall C19	B29F	1994	Ex Star Line, 1995
110	H404BVR	Mercedes-Benz 814D	Carlyle	C29F	1991	Ex Star Line, 1995
111	D211SKD	Mercedes-Benz L608D	Reeve Burgess	B20F	1986	

112-119 — Mercedes-Benz L608D — Alexander AM — B20F — 1986

112	D212SKD	114	D214SKD	116	D216SKD	118	D221SKD	119	D219SKD
113	D213SKD	115	D225SKD	117	D217SKD				

120-129 — Mercedes-Benz 709D — Alexander Sprint — B29F — 1995

120	M120YCM	122	M122YCM	124	M124YCM	126	M126YCM	128	M128YCM
121	M121YCM	123	M123YCM	125	M125YCM	127	M127YCM	129	M129YCM

130-134 — Mercedes-Benz 709D — Reeve Burgess Beaver — B27F* — 1992 — Ex Star Line, 1995; *131/2 are B29F

130	J296NNB	131	J297NNB	132	J298NNB	133	J299NNB	134	K876UDB

135-142 — Mercedes-Benz 709D — Plaxton Beaver — B27F — 1993-94 Ex Star Line, 1995

135	K878UDB	137	K882UDB	139	K887UDB	141	L642DNA	142	L643DNA
136	K879UDB	138	K884UDB	140	L641DNA				

143-149 — Mercedes-Benz 709D — Alexander Sprint — B27F — 1994-95 Ex Star Line, 1995

143	M363KVR	145	M365KVR	147	M367KVR	148	M368KVR	149	M369KVR
144	M364KVR	146	M366KVR						

Star Line joined North Western during 1995 and brought a network of services based around Altrincham and Knutsford. Pictured in Altrincham bus station is Alexander-bodied Mercedes-Benz 709D 149, M368KVR. The latest version of the Star Line livery will be white with red and blue relief in different proportions to that presently used. *Mark Bailey*

Little White Buses of Ormskirk also joined the North Western operation in 1994 and brought into the fleet a variety of bodywork styles on Mercedes-Benz 709D minibuses. Pictured here is a Marshall-bodied example, 197, M998XRF. *Paul Wigan*

Much-travelled vehicles in the North Western fleet are three Scania K93s with Plaxton Derwent bus bodywork. Now in Liverline livery 392, G612CFA was new to Happy Days before moving to the Tellus operation of Midland Red. The trio then headed to Manchester with the Bee Line operation consequently entering the North Western fleet. *Richard Godfrey*

171	M385KVR	Mercedes-Benz 709D	Alexander Sprint	B27F	1995	Ex Wigan Bus Company, 1995
172	M392KVR	Mercedes-Benz 709D	Alexander Sprint	B27F	1995	Ex Wigan Bus Company, 1995
173	M393KVR	Mercedes-Benz 709D	Alexander Sprint	B27F	1994	Ex Wigan Bus Company, 1995
174	M394KVR	Mercedes-Benz 709D	Alexander Sprint	B27F	1995	Ex Wigan Bus Company, 1995
189	M239XLV	Iveco TurboDaily 59.10	Marshall C31	B27F	1995	Ex Little White Buses, 1995
190	M240XLV	Iveco TurboDaily 59.10	Marshall C31	B27F	1995	Ex Little White Buses, 1995
191	K457EVC	Mercedes-Benz 811D	Dormobile Routemaker	B31F	1993	Ex Little White Buses, 1995
192	K787VNR	Mercedes-Benz 811D	Wright	B33F	1993	Ex Little White Buses, 1995
193	L193DBC	Mercedes-Benz 811D	Marshall C16	B31F	1994	Ex Little White Buses, 1995
194	L529XVR	Mercedes-Benz 811D	Dormobile Routemaker	B31F	1993	Ex Little White Buses, 1995
195	M689FJF	Mercedes-Benz 811D	Marshall C16	B31F	1994	Ex Little White Buses, 1995
196	M615XLG	Mercedes-Benz 811D	Marshall C16	B31F	1994	Ex Little White Buses, 1995
197	M998XRF	Mercedes-Benz 811D	Marshall C16	B31F	1995	Ex Little White Buses, 1995
198	H81PTG	Mercedes-Benz 811D	Optare StarRider	B33F	1991	Ex Wigan Bus Company, 1995
199	H85PTG	Mercedes-Benz 811D	Optare StarRider	B33F	1991	Ex Wigan Bus Company, 1995

200-210

Leyland National 10351A/2R — B44F — 1979-80 Ex Parfitt's, 1995

200	BYW359V	203	BYW402V	205	BYW412V	207	BYW427V	209	BYW432V
201	BYW367V	204	BYW406V	206	BYW413V	208	BYW430V	210	BYW437V
202	BYW379V								

213	MLJ919P	Leyland National 11351A/1R				B49F	1976	Ex Maidstone & District, 1995
214	MAR781P	Leyland National 11351A/1R				B49F	1976	Ex Maidstone & District, 1995

215-255

Leyland National 11351A/1R — B49F — 1976-78 Ex Ribble, 1986

215	SCK688P	222	SCK700P	236	UHG759R	242	ACW765R	249	CBV787S
216	SCK689P	225	SCK706P	237	UHG760R	243	CBV766S	250	CBV791S
218	SCK692P	226	SCK710P	238	ACW761R	244	CBV767S	251	CBV792S
219	SCK693P	229	UHG724R	239	ACW762R	246	CBV773S	252	CBV793S
220	SCK698P	231	UHG735R	240	ACW763R	247	CBV774S	253	CBV794S
221	SCK699P	234	UHG751R	241	ACW764R	248	CBV786S	255	CBV796S

256	JOX515P	Leyland National 11351A/1R	B49F	1976	Ex Midland Red North, 1988
257	JOX520P	Leyland National 11351A/1R	B49F	1976	Ex Midland Red North, 1988
258	NOE592R	Leyland National 11351A/1R	B49F	1977	Ex Midland Red North, 1988
259	UTU980R	Leyland National 11351A/1R	B49F	1977	Ex Crosville, 1989
260	JOX522P	Leyland National 11351A/1R	B49F	1976	Ex Midland, 1995
261	LRB202W	Leyland National 2 NL116L11/2R	B52F	1980	Ex West Riding, 1995
262	AFM2W	Leyland National 2 NL116AL11/2R	B52F	1981	Ex Crosville, 1989
263	AFM3W	Leyland National 2 NL116AL11/2R	B52F	1981	Ex Crosville, 1989
264	AFM4W	Leyland National 2 NL116AL11/2R	B52F	1981	Ex Crosville, 1989
267	FCA7X	Leyland National 2 NL116AL11/2R	B52F	1982	Ex Crosville, 1989
275	BVP811V	Leyland National 2 NL116L11/1R	B49F	1980	Ex Midland Red North, 1988
277	CCY817V	Leyland National 2 NL116L11/1R	B52F	1980	Ex West Riding, 1995
278	EON823V	Leyland National 2 NL116L11/1R	B49F	1980	Ex Midland Red North, 1988
280	FCA10X	Leyland National 2 NL116AL11/2R(6HLXB)	B52F	1982	Ex Crosville, 1989
281	NTU11Y	Leyland National 2 NL116HLXB/2R	B52F	1983	Ex Crosville, 1989
282	NTU12Y	Leyland National 2 NL116HLXB/2R	B52F	1983	Ex Crosville, 1989
283	NTU13Y	Leyland National 2 NL116HLXB/2R	B52F	1983	Ex Crosville, 1989
284	NTU15Y	Leyland National 2 NL116HLXB/2R	B52F	1983	Ex Crosville, 1989
289	PKP551R	Leyland National 11351A/1R	B49F	1977	Ex Maidstone & District, 1995
290	VKE561S	Leyland National 11351A/1R	B49F	1977	Ex Maidstone & District, 1995
291	PUP505T	Leyland National 11351A/1R	B49F	1979	Ex Maidstone & District, 1995
294	KNV514P	Leyland National 11351/1R	B49F	1976	Ex Midland Fox, 1994
295	PUK638R	Leyland National 11351A/1R	B49F	1977	Ex Midland Fox, 1994
296	PUK640R	Leyland National 11351A/1R	B49F	1977	Ex Midland Fox, 1994
298	HFM186N	Leyland National 11351/1R/SC	B48F	1975	Ex Crosville, 1989
301	DBV845W	Leyland National 2 NL106L11/1R	B44F	1980	Ex Ribble, 1986
303	JCK851W	Leyland National 2 NL106AL11/1R	B44F	1981	Ex Ribble, 1986
306	LFR854X	Leyland National 2 NL106AL11/1R	B44F	1981	Ex Ribble, 1986
309	LFR867X	Leyland National 2 NL106AL11/1R	B44F	1981	Ex Ribble, 1986
310	LFR869X	Leyland National 2 NL106AL11/1R	B44F	1981	Ex Ribble, 1986
311	NPK250R	Leyland National 10351A/1R	B41F	1976	Ex Northumbria, 1994
312	NPK263R	Leyland National 10351A/1R	B41F	1977	Ex Northumbria, 1995
313	LPB196P	Leyland National 10351/1R	B39F	1976	Ex Northumbria, 1995
314	BPL476T	Leyland National 10351B/1R	B41F	1979	Ex Northumbria, 1995
315	BPL486T	Leyland National 10351B/1R	B41F	1979	Ex Northumbria, 1995
319	YFY1M	Leyland National 1151/2R	B49F	1974	Ex Preston, 1990
320	GHU643N	Leyland National 10351/1R	B44F	1975	Ex Crosville, 1989

321	NPK233R	Leyland National 10351A/1R			B41F	1976	Ex Luton & District, 1995
322	LPB207P	Leyland National 10351/1R			B41F	1976	Ex London & Country, 1989
323	LPB195P	Leyland National 10351/1R			B39F	1976	Ex London & Country, 1989
324	LPB205P	Leyland National 10351/1R			B41F	1976	Ex London & Country, 1989
325	LPB225P	Leyland National 10351/1R			B41F	1976	Ex London & Country, 1989
326	NPK259R	Leyland National 10351A/1R			B41F	1976	Ex Northumbria, 1995
328	LPB209P	Leyland National 10351/1R			B41F	1976	Ex London & Country, 1989
329	LPB219P	Leyland National 10351/1R			B41F	1976	Ex London & Country, 1989

331-340

Leyland National 10351A/1R — B41F — 1976-77 Ex London & Country, 1989
333 ex Northumbria, 1995; 338 ex Luton & District, 1994

331	NPK242R	333	NPK258R	335	UPB301S	338	UPB342S	340	UPB335S
332	NPK245R	334	SPC279R	336	UPB322S	339	UPB334S		

341-345

Leyland National 10351B/1R — B44F — 1978-79 Ex Crosville, 1989

341	HMA567T	342	HMA568T	343	JTU582T	344	JTU583T	345	EMB643S

346	YPL408T	Leyland National 10351B/1R			B41F	1978	Ex Luton & District, 1994

347-352

Leyland National 10351B/1R — B44F — 1978-79 Ex Crosville, 1989

347	GMB657T	349	GMB668T	350	GMB670T	351	MCA675T	352	MCA678T
348	GMB663T								

353	YPL455T	Leyland National 10351B/1R			B41F	1979	Ex Luton & District, 1994
354	ODM680V	Leyland National 10351B/1R (6HLX)			B44F	1979	Ex Crosville, 1989
355	YPL399T	Leyland National 10351B/1R			B41F	1978	Ex LNorthumbria, 1995

356-373

Leyland National 11351A/1R (6HLX) — B49F — 1977-79 Ex Crosville, 1990

356	CFM350S	361	EMB367S	365	GMB384T	368	KMA395T	371	KMA403T
357	CFM351S	362	GMB375T	366	GMB385T	369	KMA396T	372	KMA412T
359	EMB360S	363	GMB379T	367	GMB386T	370	KMA400T	373	YTU986S
360	EMB366S	364	GMB380T						

374	GMB392T	Leyland National 11351A/1R(6HLX)			B49F	1978	Ex C-Line, 1993
375	KMA397T	Leyland National 11351A/1R(6HLX)			B49F	1979	Ex C-Line, 1993
376	GMB666T	Leyland National 10351B/1R			B44F	1978	Ex Midland, 1995
377	GMB667T	Leyland National 10351B/1R			B44F	1978	Ex Midland, 1995
378	BPL495T	Leyland National 10351B/1R			B41F	1979	Ex Midland, 1995
379	HMA559T	Leyland National 10351B/1R			B44F	1978	Ex Midland, 1995

381-388

Dennis Falcon SDA421 — East Lancashire EL2000 — B48F — 1990

381	G381EKA	383	G383EKA	385	G385EKA	387	G387EKA	388	G388EKA
382	G382EKA	384	G384EKA	386	G386EKA				

390	G610CFA	Scania K93CRB	Plaxton Derwent	B57F	1990	Ex Midland Red North, 1993
391	G611CFA	Scania K93CRB	Plaxton Derwent	B57F	1990	Ex Midland Red North, 1993
392	G612CFA	Scania K93CRB	Plaxton Derwent	B57F	1990	Ex Midland Red North, 1993
393	G41HKY	Scania K93CRB	Plaxton Derwent	B57F	1990	Ex Stevensons, 1994
394	D164UTO	Scania K92CRB	East Lancashire	B51F	1986	Ex Stevensons, 1994
395	D163WTV	Scania K92CRB	East Lancashire	B51F	1987	Ex Stevensons, 1994
396	GDM996X	Leyland Leopard PSU5/4R	Willowbrook Warrior (1992)	B52F	1982	Ex Liverline, 1993
397	L532EHD	DAF SB220LC550	Ikarus CitiBus	B48F	1994	Ex Wigan Bus Company, 1995
398	L533EHD	DAF SB220LC550	Ikarus CitiBus	B48F	1994	Ex Wigan Bus Company, 1995
399	790NWC	Leyland National 11351A/1R		DP50DL	1976	Ex Ribble, 1986

400-409

Leyland National 11351/1R (DAF) — B50F — 1974 Ex West Midlands Travel, 1995

400	TOE468N	402	TOE486N	404	TOE488N	406	TOE490N	408	TOE497N
401	TOE469N	403	TOE487N	405	TOE489N	407	TOE491N	409	TOE498N

487	RFR409P	Leyland Atlantean AN68/1R	Eastern Coach Works	H43/31F	1976	Ex Ribble, 1991
489	RFR423P	Leyland Atlantean AN68/1R	Eastern Coach Works	H43/31F	1976	Ex Ribble, 1991
491	SFV433P	Leyland Atlantean AN68/1R	Eastern Coach Works	H43/31F	1976	Ex Ribble, 1991
500	TRN466V	Leyland Atlantean AN68A/1R	Eastern Coach Works	H43/31F	1979	Ex Ribble, 1986

Leigh Line is one of the smaller operational units within the area served by the North Western fleet. Shown here is 312, NPK263R one of several of the shorter 10-metre length of the Leyland National now operating for the group. *Gerry Mead*

The eight Dennis Falcons have now moved to Manchester where they have received Bee Line livery. Pictured heading for Stalybridge on the Ashton New Road service is 387, G387EKA. *Mike Fowler*

For a while the North Western livery comprised blue and red which, as shown in this mono picture, presented a dark scheme. More recent repaints have incorporated the colours on a yellow base - as shown in the colour plates. Here we see Eastern Coach Works-bodied Leyland Atlantean 510, FBV495W from a batch that has just seen its first sales. *Richard Godfrey*

501-530

Leyland Atlantean AN68B/1R   Eastern Coach Works   H43/31F   1980-81   Ex Ribble, 1986

501	FBV486W	507	FBV492W	513	FBV498W	521	FBV506W	526	FBV511W
502	FBV487W	508	FBV493W	514	FBV499W	522	FBV507W	527	FBV512W
503	FBV488W	509	FBV494W	515	FBV500W	523	FBV508W	528	FBV513W
504	FBV489W	510	FBV495W	518	FBV503W	524	FBV509W	529	FBV514W
505	FBV490W	511	FBV496W	519	FBV504W	525	FBV510W	530	FBV515W
506	FBV491W	512	FBV497W	520	FBV505W				

531	RFR414P	Leyland Atlantean AN68/1R	Eastern Coach Works	H43/31F	1976	Ex Ribble, 1993
532	SFV427P	Leyland Atlantean AN68/1R	Eastern Coach Works	H43/31F	1976	Ex Bee Line Buzz, 1993
533	SFV428P	Leyland Atlantean AN68/1R	Eastern Coach Works	H43/31F	1976	Ex Bee Line Buzz, 1993
534	SFV432P	Leyland Atlantean AN68/1R	Eastern Coach Works	H43/31F	1976	Ex Ribble, 1993
535	SFV436P	Leyland Atlantean AN68/1R	Eastern Coach Works	H43/31F	1976	Ex Ribble, 1993
536	NNO65P	Leyland Atlantean AN68A/1R	Eastern Coach Works	H43/31F	1976	Ex Bee Line Buzz, 1993
537	TPU70R	Leyland Atlantean AN68A/1R	Eastern Coach Works	H43/31F	1977	Ex Colchester, 1992
538	TPU72R	Leyland Atlantean AN68A/1R	Eastern Coach Works	H43/31F	1977	Ex C-Line, 1993

543-563

Bristol VRT/SL3/501   Eastern Coach Works   H43/31F*   1978-81   Ex Crosville, 1989-90
*545/7/4/50/3/63 are H43/30F

543	RMA437V	546	PCA424V	549	WTU499W	552	FTU386T	558	RMA439V
544	PCA422V	547	PCA425V	550	BTU374S	553	FTU391T	562	WTU496W
545	PCA423V	548	RLG427V	551	FTU382T	554	JMB406T	563	WTU497W

564-568

Bristol VRT/SL3/6LXB   Eastern Coach Works   H43/31F*   1980   Ex Crosville, 1989
*566/8 are H43/30F

564	VCA453W	565	VCA454W	566	VCA455W	567	VCA456W	568	VCA463W

569	WTU479W	Bristol VRT/SL3/6LXC(6LXB)	Eastern Coach Works	H43/30F	1981	Ex Crosville, 1990
570	WTU480W	Bristol VRT/SL3/6LXC(6LXB)	Eastern Coach Works	H43/30F	1981	Ex Crosville, 1990

The latest City Express livery is shown here on Dennis Dominator 630, F630BKD, the first of the 1989 batch of Dominators which carry East Lancashire express bodies. Production of the Dennis Dominator is now at an end, with the final chassis destined for London & Country now at the bodybuilders. *Paul Wigan*

600-625

Leyland Olympian ONLXB/1R Eastern Coach Works H45/32F 1983-85 Ex Ribble, 1986

600	DBV133Y	605	A141MRN	610	B149TRN	615	B155TRN	621	B965WRN
601	DBV135Y	606	A144OFR	611	B150TRN	616	B960WRN	622	B966WRN
602	DBV136Y	607	A146OFR	612	B151TRN	618	B962WRN	623	B967WRN
603	A139MRN	608	A147OFR	613	B153TRN	619	B963WRN	624	B968WRN
604	A140MRN	609	B148TRN	614	B154TRN	620	B964WRN	625	B969WRN

626	G626EKA	Dennis Dominator DDA1031	East Lancashire	H47/29F	1990
627	G627EKA	Dennis Dominator DDA1031	East Lancashire	H47/29F	1990
628	G628EKA	Dennis Dominator DDA1031	East Lancashire	H47/29F	1990
629	G629EKA	Dennis Dominator DDA1031	East Lancashire	H47/29F	1990

630-635

Dennis Dominator DDA1026 East Lancashire DPH43/25F 1989

630	F630BKD	632	F632BKD	633	F633BKD	634	F634BKD	635	F635BKD
631	F631BKD							

636	F636BKD	Dennis Dominator DDA1025	East Lancashire	H45/31F	1989
637	F637BKD	Dennis Dominator DDA1025	East Lancashire	H45/31F	1989
638	F638BKD	Dennis Dominator DDA1025	East Lancashire	H45/31F	1989
639	F639BKD	Dennis Dominator DDA1025	East Lancashire	H45/31F	1989

640-653

Volvo Citybus B10M-50 East Lancashire H49/39F 1989-90

640	G640CHF	643	G643CHF	646	G661DTJ	649	G649EKA	652	G652EKA
641	G641CHF	644	G659DTJ	647	G647EKA	650	G650EKA	653	G653EKA
642	G642CHF	645	G660DTJ	648	G648EKA	651	G651EKA		

654-662

Leyland Olympian ONLXB/1R Eastern Coach Works H45/32F 1983-84 Ex Crosville, 1989

654	PFM126Y	656	PFM129Y	658	A140SMA	660	A149UDM	662	A153UDM
655	PFM128Y	657	A139SMA	659	A141SMA	661	A151UDM		

663	G663FKA	Dennis Dominator DDA1031	East Lanacshire	H47/29F	1990	
664	G664FKA	Dennis Dominator DDA1031	East Lanacshire	H47/29F	1990	
665	G665FKA	Dennis Dominator DDA1031	East Lanacshire	H47/29F	1990	
666	G667FKA	Dennis Dominator DDA1031	East Lanacshire	H47/29F	1990	
667	GFM110X	Leyland Olympian ONLXB/1R	Eastern Coach Works	H45/32F	1982	Ex Crosville, 1989
668	A142SMA	Leyland Olympian ONLXB/1R	Eastern Coach Works	H45/32F	1983	Ex Crosville, 1989
669	A148SMA	Leyland Olympian ONLXB/1R	Eastern Coach Works	H45/32F	1983	Ex Crosville, 1989
670	A147SMA	Leyland Olympian ONLXB/1R	Eastern Coach Works	H45/32F	1983	Ex Crosville, 1989

671-680

Scania N113DRB Northern Counties H47/33F 1990-91 Ex Liverline, 1993

| 671 | G34HKY | 673 | G36HKY | 675 | G38HKY | 677 | G714LKW | 679 | H804RWJ |
| 672 | G35HKY | 674 | G37HKY | 676 | G711LKW | 678 | H803RWJ | 680 | H805RWJ |

711	SCD731N	Leyland Atlantean AN68/1R	Park Royal	H43/30F	1974	Ex London & Country, 1989
720	OCO107S	Leyland Atlantean AN68A/1R	Roe	H43/30F	1978	Ex Plymouth, 1990
721	UPK125S	Leyland Atlantean AN68A/1R	Park Royal	H43/30F	1978	Ex London & Country, 1991
724	UPK141S	Leyland Atlantean AN68A/1R	Park Royal	H43/30F	1978	Ex London & Country, 1991
725	OCO109S	Leyland Atlantean AN68A/1R	Roe	H43/30F	1978	Ex Plymouth, 1990
727	UPK137S	Leyland Atlantean AN68A/1R	Park Royal	H43/30F	1978	Ex London & Country, 1991
728	UPK138S	Leyland Atlantean AN68A/1R	Park Royal	H43/30F	1978	Ex London & Country, 1991
729	UPK140S	Leyland Atlantean AN68A/1R	Park Royal	H43/30F	1978	Ex London & Country, 1991
730	VPA150S	Leyland Atlantean AN68A/1R	Park Royal	H43/30F	1978	Ex London & Country, 1991
737	XPG166T	Leyland Atlantean AN68A/1R	Park Royal	H43/30F	1978	Ex Luton & District, 1992
739	XPG169T	Leyland Atlantean AN68A/1R	Park Royal	H43/30F	1978	Ex Luton & District, 1991
741	XPG171T	Leyland Atlantean AN68A/1R	Park Royal	H43/30F	1978	Ex Luton & District, 1992
742	XPG177T	Leyland Atlantean AN68A/1R	Park Royal	H43/30F	1978	Ex London & Country, 1991
744	XPG181T	Leyland Atlantean AN68A/1R	Park Royal	H43/30F	1978	Ex London & Country, 1991
745	XPG193T	Leyland Atlantean AN68A/1R	Roe	H43/30F	1979	Ex London & Country, 1991
750	EPH230V	Leyland Atlantean AN68A/1R	Roe	H43/30F	1980	Ex London & Country, 1991

767-775

MCW Metrobus DR102 MCW H43/30F 1981-82 On Hire from West Midlands Travel

| 767 | LOA430X | 770 | GOG257W | 772 | LOA426X | 774 | LOA435X | 775 | KJW284W |
| 768 | KJW281W | 771 | GOG259W | 773 | LOA428X | | | | |

| 776 | 776DYE | AEC Routemaster R2RH | Park Royal | H36/28R | 1963 | Ex GM Buses, 1990 |

777-817

MCW Metrobus DR102 MCW H43/30F 1980-82 On Hire from West Midlands Travel

777	BOK32V	784	BOK65V	792	GOG137W	801	LOA434X	808	GOG161W
778	BOK33V	786	BOK77V	794	GOG141W	802	BOK34V	810	GOG248W
779	BOK36V	787	BOK78V	795	GOG144W	803	BOK26V	811	GOG263W
780	BOK50V	788	BOK79V	797	LOA332X	804	BOK40V	812	GOG266W
781	BOK51V	789	BOK90V	798	LOA416X	805	BOK54V	815	LOA432X
782	BOK52V	790	GOG99V	799	LOA419X	806	BOK67V	816	KJW287W
783	BOK53V	791	GOG116W	800	LOA420X	807	GOG159W	817	KJW288W

818	OMA510V	Leyland Leopard PSU3E/4R	Duple Dominant II Express	C49F	1979	Ex Crosville, 1990
840	K200SLT	Dennis Javelin 12SDA2117	Berkhof Excellence 1000 L	C51FT	1993	Ex Star Line, 1995
842	M2SLT	Scania K113CRB	Irizar Century	C49FT	1995	Ex Star Line, 1995
843	L3SLT	Dennis Javelin 10SDA2119	Berkhof Excellence 1000 L	C39FT	1993	Ex Star Line, 1995
844	K100SLT	Dennis Javelin 10SDA2119	Berkhof Excellence 1000 L	C36FT	1993	Ex Star Line, 1995
857	G644EVN	CVE Omni	CVE	B15FL	1990	Ex Greater Manchester PTE, 1994
881	838AFM	Bristol Lodekka LD6G	Eastern Coach Works	H33/27R	1957	Ex Driver trainer, 1993
890	K890UDB	Toyota Coaster HDB30R	Caetano Optimo II	C18F	1992	Ex Star Line, 1995
933	JFM220D	Bristol Lodekka LD6G	Eastern Coach Works	H33/27R	1966	Ex Crosville, 1989

Inherited from Liverline were ten Scania N113 double-deck buses with Northern Counties Palatine bodywork. These were new to that operation and are still allocated there and shown here is 672, G35HKY.
The latest livery for Bee Line, North Western, Leigh Line, The Wigan Bus Company and Runcorn Busway operation is shown on 801, LOA434X. One of a batch of MCW Metrobus double-decks on extended loan from West Midlands Travel it is seen displaying the scheme shortly after its formal launch.

The latest arrivals with North Western are five Scania low-floor L113 buses with Wright Axcess Ultralow bodies for service within Greater Manchester. Allocated to the Star Line operation they may be found on Altrincham local services. Seen heading for Bowden Vale in its first week of operation is 1002, N102YVU. *Bill Potter*

1001-1005

		Scania L113CRL		Wright Axcess Ultraflow		B48F*		1996		*1001 is B42F
1001	N101YVU	1002	N102YVU	1003	N103YVU	1004	N104YVU	1005	N105YVU	

1150	L150SBG	Dennis Dart 9SDL3034	East Lancashire	B32F	1993		
1151	L151SBG	Dennis Dart 9SDL3034	East Lancashire	B32F	1993		
1152	L152SBG	Dennis Dart 9SDL3034	East Lancashire	B32F	1993		
1153	L153UKB	Dennis Dart 9SDL3034	Plaxton Pointer	B20F	1994		
1154	L154UKB	Dennis Dart 9SDL3034	Plaxton Pointer	B20F	1994		
1155	L155UKB	Dennis Dart 9SDL3034	Plaxton Pointer	B20F	1994		
1156	L156UKB	Dennis Dart 9SDL3034	Plaxton Pointer	B20F	1994		

1157-1170

		Dennis Dart 9.8SDL3040*		East Lancashire		B40F		1994-95 1170 is 9.8SDL3054	
1157	M157WKA	1160	M160WKA	1163	M163WKA	1166	M166WKA	1169	M169WKA
1158	M158WKA	1161	M161WKA	1164	M164WKA	1167	M167WKA	1170	M170WKA
1159	M159WKA	1162	M162WKA	1165	M165WKA	1168	M168WKA		

1171-1187

		Dennis Dart 9.8SDL3040		Plaxton Pointer		B40F		1995	
1171	M171YKA	1175	M175YKA	1179	M179YKA	1182	M182YKA	1185	M185YKA
1172	M172YKA	1176	M176YKA	1180	M180YKA	1183	M183YKA	1186	M186YKA
1173	M173YKA	1177	M177YKA	1181	M181YKA	1184	M184YKA	1187	M187YKA
1174	M174YKA	1178	M178YKA						

1188-1199

		Dennis Dart 9.8SDL3054		Plaxton Pointer		B40F		1995	
1188	M188YKA	1191	M191YKA	1194	M194YKA	1196	M196YKA	1198	M198YKA
1189	M189YKA	1192	M192YKA	1195	M195YKA	1197	M197YKA	1199	M199YKA
1190	M190YKA	1193	M193YKA						

Opposite: **Dennis Darts form the mainstay of the midi-bus requirement with examples bodied by Plaxton, Northern Counties and East Lancashire present in the fleet. Shown here are 1266, M370KVR with Northern Counties bodywork in Star Line colours and 1159, M159WKA, an East Lancashire example in Runcorn Busways livery and photographed before the type was renumbered into their current series.**

1201-1210

Dennis Lance 11SDA3113 — Plaxton Verde — B49F — 1995

1201	M201YKA	**1203**	M203YKA	**1205**	M205YKA	**1207**	M207YKA	**1209**	M209YKA
1202	M202YKA	**1204**	M204YKA	**1206**	M206YKA	**1208**	M208YKA	**1210**	M210YKA

1211	M211YKD	Dennis Dart 9.8SDL3040	Plaxton Pointer	B40F	1995
1212	M212YKD	Dennis Dart 9.8SDL3040	Plaxton Pointer	B40F	1995
1213	M213YKD	Dennis Dart 9.8SDL3040	Plaxton Pointer	B40F	1995
1214	M214YKD	Dennis Dart 9.8SDL3054	Plaxton Pointer	B40F	1995
1215	M215YKD	Dennis Dart 9.8SDL3054	Plaxton Pointer	B40F	1995
1216	M216YKD	Dennis Dart 9.8SDL3054	Plaxton Pointer	B40F	1995

1217-1264

Dennis Dart 9.8SDL3054 — East Lancashire — B40F — 1995

1217	M217AKB	**1227**	M227AKB	**1237**	N237CKA	**1247**	N247CKA	**1256**	N256CKA
1218	M218AKB	**1228**	M228AKB	**1238**	N238CKA	**1248**	N248CKA	**1257**	N257CKA
1219	M219AKB	**1229**	M229AKB	**1239**	N239CKA	**1249**	N249CKA	**1258**	N258CKA
1220	M220AKB	**1230**	M230AKB	**1240**	N240CKA	**1250**	N250CKA	**1259**	N259CKA
1221	M221AKB	**1231**	M231AKB	**1241**	N241CKA	**1251**	N251CKA	**1260**	N260CKA
1222	M322AKB	**1232**	M232AKB	**1242**	N242CKA	**1252**	N252CKA	**1261**	N261CKA
1223	M223AKB	**1233**	N233CKA	**1243**	N243CKA	**1253**	N253CKA	**1262**	N262CKA
1224	M224AKB	**1234**	N234CKA	**1244**	N244CKA	**1254**	N254CKA	**1263**	N263CKA
1225	M225AKB	**1235**	N235CKA	**1245**	N245CKA	**1255**	N255CKA	**1264**	N264CKA
1226	M226AKB	**1236**	N236CKA	**1246**	N246CKA				

1265	K877UDB	Dennis Dart 9.8SDL3017	Plaxton Pointer	B40F	1992	Ex Star Line, 1995
1266	M370KVR	Dennis Dart 9.8SDL3035	Northern Counties Paladin	B40F	1994	Ex Star Line, 1995
1267	M371KVR	Dennis Dart 9.8SDL3035	Northern Counties Paladin	B40F	1994	Ex Star Line, 1995
1268	M372KVR	Dennis Dart 9.8SDL3035	Northern Counties Paladin	B40F	1994	Ex Star Line, 1995
1269	M841RCP	Dennis Dart 9.8SDL3054	Northern Counties Paladin II	B39F	1995	Ex Wigan Bus Company, 1995
1270	M842RCP	Dennis Dart 9.8SDL3054	Northern Counties Paladin II	B39F	1995	Ex Wigan Bus Company, 1995
1271	M843RCP	Dennis Dart 9.8SDL3054	Northern Counties Paladin II	B39F	1995	Ex Wigan Bus Company, 1995

Previous Registrations:

790NWC   SCK691P   GDM996X   VUR217J

Livery: Yellow, blue and red (North Western, Bee Line, Leigh Line, Runcorn Busway and The Wigan Bus Company); White, blue and red (Star Line); white and blue (Liverbus and Little White Buses); white (Warrington Goldline).

Operational Allocations:

Bee Line (Manchester): 6/9/11/9/9/21/4/6-8/37/42/6, 70/2/3/5/6/9/82/8/9/93-5/99, 100/20-5, 382/5-7, 402/5/7/8, 601/4-7/13/21/2/5/54-6/8-62/7-70, 767/8/71/2/4/5/7/8/82/4/6/8/90/2/7, 800/2/3/6/8/11/2/5/-7

Leigh Line (Leigh): 61, 74/8, 241-4/50/1/6/90/1, 311/2/20/1/6.

Little White Buses (Ormskirk):

Liverline: 390-3, 502/30/8, 600/2/3/6-12/4-6/8-20/3/4/7/71-80, 711/20/4/5/7-30/7/9/41/2/4/50

Runcorn Busway: 215/9/20/2/9/37/48/53/5/60/94/6/8, 313/5/9/33/8/46/8/9/54/5/9-61/75-9/81/3/4/8, 780/7, 804/7, 1157-70, 1201-4.

Star Line (Knutsford): 69/77/96-8, 106-10/30-49, 840-4/90, 954, 1265-8

Warrington Gold Line: 3/4, 10/6/31/9/45/51/2/64-7, 101/12/26-9, 342-4/7/50-2, 770/3/9/81/3/9/91/4/5/8/9, 810, 1171-99, 1205-16

Wigan Bus Company (Wigan): 13, 58-60/80, 111/3-5/7-9/71-4/98/9, 263/4/7/75/8/80/2-4, 301/3/6/9/10/97/8, 510-5, 857, 1153-6, 1269-71.

North Western: remainder.

NOVA SCOTIA TRAVEL

A Gilligan & B Wilson, Unit 9 Woodford Ind Est, Browning Way,
Winsford, Cheshire, CW7 2RB

GNV659N	Leyland National 11351/1R		B49F	1974	Ex Luton & District, 1995
NOE557R	Leyland National 11351/1R		B49F	1976	Ex London & Country, 1995
JBR687T	Leyland National 11351A/1R		B49F	1978	Ex Northumbria, 1995
EPD534V	Leyland National 10351B/1R		B41F	1979	Ex Kentish Bus, 1995
A268POW	Iveco Daily 35.8	Robin Hood	M12	1983	
A463SBK	Iveco Daily 35.8	Robin Hood	M12	1984	
B807OVT	Iveco Daily 35.8	Robin Hood	M12	1985	
D21RPP	Iveco Daily 49.10	Robin Hood City Nippy	B21F	1987	Ex The Shires, 1995
D25RPP	Iveco Daily 49.10	Robin Hood City Nippy	B21F	1987	Ex Hawksworth, Birkenhead, 1995
E525DCU	Mercedes-Benz 307D	Devon Conversions	M9L	1987	Ex ??, 1995
E790SJA	Renault-Dodge S56	Northern Counties	B20F	1987	Ex GMN, 1995
E688WNE	Peugeot-Talbot Express	Made-to-Measure	M14	1988	
E706WNE	Peugeot-Talbot Express	Made-to-Measure	M14	1988	
F518HUS	Peugeot-Talbot Freeway	Talbot	B17FL	1989	Ex Marbill, Beith, 1995
F448LBA	Peugeot-Talbot Pullman	Talbot	B20F	1989	
F481SDU	Peugeot-Talbot Pullman	Talbot	B22F	1989	Ex Primrose, Leominster, 1992
G995LAH	Peugeot-Talbot Pullman	Talbot	B22F	1990	Ex Constance, Swaffham, 1994
H903YUS	Peugeot-Talbot Freeway	Talbot	DP12FL	1990	Ex Clydeside, 1995
H904YUS	Peugeot-Talbot Freeway	Talbot	DP12FL	1990	Ex Clydeside, 1995
H905YUS	Peugeot-Talbot Freeway	Talbot	DP12FL	1990	Ex Clydeside, 1995

Livery: White and red

Leaving Northwich on a new commercial service is F448LBA of Nova Scotia. This Talbot tri-axle carries the later white and red livery. Recently, the operator has increased the number of Cheshire Bus journeys now operated in the area. *Bill Potter*

OGDEN'S

J D Ogden, Baxter's Lane, Sutton, St Helens, Merseyside

HFF234	AEC Reliance 6U3ZR	Plaxton Supreme IV	C53F	1979	Ex Harding, Halebank, 1984
OIJ2645	Leyland Leopard PSU3B/4R	Duple Dominant IV	C49F	1982	Ex Mercer, Longridge, 1987
HIL6956	Leyland Tiger TLCTL11/2R	Plaxton Supreme V	C46F	1982	Ex SUT, Sheffield, 1987
DOI9172	DAF SB2300DHS585	Plaxton Paramount 3200 II	C53F	1986	
HIL2381	DAF MB230LT615	Van Hool Alizée	C55FT	1987	Ex Ardenvale, Knowle, 1991
E909EAY	DAF MB230DKFL615	Plaxton Paramount 3200 III	C57F	1987	Ex Dennis's, Ashton-u-Lyne, 1994
JOI2949	DAF SB2305DHS585	Van Hool Alizée	C51FT	1988	Ex Wood, Barnsley, 1995
E759HJF	Mercedes-Benz L307D	Yeates	M12	1988	
470DOT	DAF MB230LB615	Plaxton Paramount 3500 III	C53F	1988	Ex Smiths, Alcester, 1990
F660OHD	DAF SB2305DHTD585	Plaxton Paramount 3200 II	C53F	1988	Ex Sweyne, Swinefleet, 1992
F215RJX	DAF MB230LB615	Plaxton Paramount 3500 III	C53F	1989	
G228HCP	DAF MB230LT615	Plaxton Paramount 3500 III	C53F	1990	
J136OBU	Peugeot-Talbot Express	Made-to-Measure	M12	1992	
K333DOT	DAF SB3000DKVF601	Van Hool Alizée	C51FT	1993	
L10GGY	Ford Transit VE6	Deansgate	M14	1993	
M252SRN	Ford Transit VE6	Ford	M8	1995	

Previous Registrations:

470DOT	E641KCX	HIL2381	D618YCX	K333DOT	K540RJX
DOI9172	C631TUT, COI6771	HIL6956	NHL261X, JOI2949	OIJ2645	RHG911X
HFF234	DCH359T	JOI2949	E644KCX		

Livery: White, red and grey

Note: Commercial services passed to MTL during 1995

Since the days of the charabanc Blackpool has been a major attraction for the day tripper with greater numbers now heading for the town as its motorway links reduce travelling time. Pictured here is HIL6956, a Leyland Tiger, with a DAF badge, recently withdrawn from the Ogdens Travel fleet as the fleet has recently received several newer coaches. *Paul Wigan*

ROGER HILL COACHES

E R & A Hill, 6 Ennerdale Drive, Congleton, Cheshire, CW12 4FR

CRE791M	Daimler Fleetline CRG6LXB	Willowbrook	H43/33F	1977	Ex Lonsdale, Heysham, 1986
KEH976N	Daimler Fleetline CRL6	Park Royal	H43/33F	1977	Ex West Midlands Travel, 1990
HIL3073	Leyland Leopard PSU3C/4R	Plaxton Supreme III Express	C53F	1976	Ex Trent, 1995
HIL3478	Leyland Leopard PSU3C/4R	Plaxton Supreme III Express	C53F	1976	Ex Trent, 1995
KBV146S	Leyland Leopard PSU5B/4R	Duple Dominant II	C51F	1981	Ex Dalybus, Eccles, 1995
TEH442W	Leyland Leopard PSU3E/4R	Duple Dominant III	C53F	1977	Ex PMT, 1992
G438GJC	Volvo B10M-60	Plaxton Expressliner	C46FT	1990	Ex Express Travel, 1994
H829AHS	Volvo B10M-60	Plaxton Paramount 3500 III	C53F	1991	Ex Park's, 1993
M3ERH	Dennis Javelin 12SDA2125	Plaxton Expressliner 2	C46FT	1995	

Previous Registrations:

CRE791M	NFA16M, HIL3073	KBV146S	WUG150S, 569AVF, BBJ202S, GSV90S, YMO379
HIL3073	MNU468P	KEH976N	GOG530N, HIL3478
HIL3478	MNU476P	TEH442W	KWG131W, HIL8670

Livery: Turquoise and white; National Express G438GJC, H829AHS, M3ERH.

Roger Hill uses two double-deck coaches on school contract work. These Daimler Fleetlines are painted in the turquoise and white livery and carry different types of body. Both are shown in this depot picture. On the left is CRE791M with a Willowbrook body to Nottingham's style though the vehicle was new to Burton-on-Trent, while on the right is an example from Park Royal that was new to West Midlands PTE. *Martin Grosberg*

SELWYNS

Selwyns Travel Ltd, Cavendish Farm Road, Weston, Runcorn, Cheshire, WA7 4LU

10	B163PRK	Mercedes-Benz L608D	Devon Conversions	C16F	1984	Ex Wincanton, London, 1988
13	D846RHS	Mercedes-Benz 609D	Devon Conversions	C19F	1987	
14	D845RHS	Mercedes-Benz 609D	Devon Conversions	C19F	1987	
15	E427ATT	Mercedes-Benz 609D	Devon Conversions	C19F	1987	
16	K3SEL	Mercedes-Benz 609D	Autobus Classique	C15F	1992	
23	F360MUT	Dennis Javelin 8.5SDL1903	Plaxton Paramount 3200 III	C30F	1988	Ex Davis, Minchinhampton, 1992
24	M390KVR	Dennis Javelin 8.5SDA2139	Berkhof Excellence 1000L	C33F	1994	Ex Star Line, Knutsford, 1995
27	D620YCX	DAF SB2300DHTD585	Plaxton Paramount 3500 III	C53F	1987	
30	TSU610	Kässbohrer Setra S215HD	Kässbohrer Tornado	C10FT	1990	Ex Hallmark, Luton, 1996
31	M799HPJ	Dennis Javelin 12SDA2134	Berkhof Excellence 1000	C49FT	1995	Ex Dennis demonstrator, 1996
32	F724JTU	Volvo B10M-60	Plaxton Paramount 3500 III	C53F	1989	
33	SEL853	Volvo B10M-60	Plaxton Paramount 3500 III	C49FT	1989	
34	F399KTU	Volvo B10M-60	Plaxton Paramount 3500 III	C49FT	1989	
35	H723VWU	Volvo B10M-60	Plaxton Paramount 3500 III	C37FT	1991	Ex Dodsworth, Boroughbridge, 1994
37	SEL36	Mercedes-Benz 0303/15RHD	Mercedes-Benz	C8FT	1987	Ex Hirst, Holmfirth, 1990
38	M366AMA	Dennis Javelin 12SDA2125	Plaxton Première 350	C48FT	1995	
39	M602BCA	Dennis Javelin 12SDA2161	Plaxton Première 350	C49FT	1995	
42	M367AMA	Dennis Javelin 12SDA2125	Plaxton Première 350	C53FT	1995	
43	K762FYG	Dennis Javelin 12SDA2114	Plaxton Première 350	C50F	1992	Ex Wallace Arnold, 1996
51	E510CHS	Van Hool TD824	Van Hool Astromega	CH14/0CT	1987	Ex Park's, 1995
54	SEL73	Auwaerter Neoplan N122/3	Auwaerter Skyliner	CH55/18CT	1988	Ex Coach Europe, Ratby, 1990
55	SEL133	Auwaerter Neoplan N122/3	Auwaerter Skyliner	CH55/18CT	1988	Ex Coach Europe, Ratby, 1991
56	SEL392	Auwaerter Neoplan N122/3	Auwaerter Skyliner	CH16/0CT	1986	Ex Silver Choice, East Kilbride, 1994
59	SEL23	Volvo B10M-53	Van Hool Astral	CH52/13CT	1988	Ex Excelsior, 1995
60	M6SEL	Dennis Javelin 12SDA2131	Plaxton Expressliner 2	C46FT	1994	
61	M7SEL	Dennis Javelin 12SDA2131	Plaxton Expressliner 2	C46FT	1994	
62	H112OON	Volvo B10M-60	Plaxton Expressliner	C46FT	1991	Ex Express Travel, Perth, 1994
63	H113OON	Volvo B10M-60	Plaxton Expressliner	C46FT	1991	Ex Express Travel, Perth, 1994
64	J910OEY	Volvo B10M-60	Plaxton Expressliner	C46FT	1991	Ex Express Travel, Perth, 1994
67	M365AMA	Dennis Javelin 12SDA2125	Plaxton Expressliner 2	C46FT	1995	
68	M255BDM	Volvo B10M-62	Plaxton Expressliner 2	C44FT	1995	
69	M441BDM	Volvo B10M-62	Plaxton Expressliner 2	C44FT	1995	

Livery: White, green, orange and blue; 60-4/7-9, are in National Express livery.

Note: 10/3/5/6, 23/4 form the Airport division and are based at Manchester International Airport; 30/7, 51/6 are 'band bus' with reduced seating, bunks and tables for pop group transport.

Previous Registrations:

SEL23	E880RPR, XEL44, E902GHO	SEL392	C180KET, C564NCA, YSV571
SEL36	D347CBC	SEL853	F725JTU
SEL73	E483YWJ	TSU610	From new
SEL133	F615CWJ		

SOUTH LANCS

South Lancashire Transport Co Ltd
Unit B, Beaufort Street, Peasley Cross, St Helens, Merseyside, WA9 3BQ

Depots: Beaufort Street, St Helens and Hoole Bridge, Chester

u	NGR683P	Bristol LH6L	Eastern Coach Works	B43F	1976	Ex Northumbria, 1995
u	PHN570R	Leyland Leopard PSU3D/2R	Duple Dominant	B53F	1976	Ex Darlington, 1995
u	PHN571R	Leyland Leopard PSU3D/2R	Duple Dominant	B49D	1976	Ex Darlington, 1995
	PHN572R	Leyland Leopard PSU3D/2R	Duple Dominant	B53F	1976	Ex Darlington, 1995
	AFB597V	Bristol LH6L	Eastern Coach Works	B43F	1980	Ex Badgerline, 1991
	LPY458W	Leyland Leopard PSU3E/4R	Duple Dominant	B55F	1981	Ex United, 1992
	LPY462W	Leyland Leopard PSU3E/4R	Duple Dominant	B55F	1981	Ex United, 1992
	UWY81X	Leyland Leopard PSU3F/4R	Duple Dominant IV Express	C49F	1981	Ex Yorkshire Rider, 1995
	49XBF	Leyland Leopard PSU3G/4R	Duple Dominant	B53F	1982	Ex A1 Service, (Dunn), 1991
	B43UCK	Leyland Tiger TRBTL11/2RP	Duple Dominant	B47F	1984	Ex Blackpool (Blue Bus), 1996
	D154THG	Leyland Tiger TRBTL11/2RP	East Lancashire	B55F	1986	Ex Lancaster, 1993
	D849LND	Renault-Dodge S56	Northern Counties	B20F	1986	Ex Clydeside, 1995
	D110OWG	Renault-Dodge S56	Reeve Burgess	B23F	1986	Ex Glossopdale, 1995
	D122OWG	Renault-Dodge S56	Reeve Burgess	B23F	1987	Ex Glossopdale, 1995
	D223NCS	Renault-Dodge S56	Alexander AM	B25F	1987	Ex Western Scottish, 1995
	D225NCS	Renault-Dodge S56	Alexander AM	B25F	1987	Ex Western Scottish, 1995
	D226NCS	Renault-Dodge S56	Alexander AM	B25F	1987	Ex Western Scottish, 1995
	D227NCS	Renault-Dodge S56	Alexander AM	B25F	1987	Ex Western Scottish, 1995
	D228NCS	Renault-Dodge S56	Alexander AM	B25F	1987	Ex Western Scottish, 1995
	D230NCS	Renault-Dodge S56	Alexander AM	B25F	1987	Ex Western Scottish, 1995
	D233NCS	Renault-Dodge S56	Alexander AM	B25F	1987	Ex Western Scottish, 1995
	D236NCS	Renault-Dodge S56	Alexander AM	B25F	1987	Ex Western Scottish, 1995
	D240NCS	Renault-Dodge S56	Alexander AM	B25F	1987	Ex Western Scottish, 1995
	D242NCS	Renault-Dodge S56	Alexander AM	B25F	1987	Ex Western Scottish, 1995
	D245NCS	Renault-Dodge S56	Alexander AM	B25F	1987	Ex Western Scottish, 1995
	D249NCS	Renault-Dodge S56	Alexander AM	B25F	1987	Ex Western Scottish, 1995
	D250NCS	Renault-Dodge S56	Alexander AM	B25F	1987	Ex Western Scottish, 1995
	D255NCS	Renault-Dodge S56	Alexander AM	B25F	1987	Ex Western Scottish, 1995
	D257NCS	Renault-Dodge S56	Alexander AM	B25F	1987	Ex Western Scottish, 1995
	D258NCS	Renault-Dodge S56	Alexander AM	B25F	1987	Ex Western Scottish, 1995
	D259NCS	Renault-Dodge S56	Alexander AM	B25F	1987	Ex Western Scottish, 1995
	D260NCS	Renault-Dodge S56	Alexander AM	B25F	1987	Ex Western Scottish, 1995
	D303SDS	Renault-Dodge S56	Alexander AM	B25F	1987	Ex Western Scottish, 1996
	D305SDS	Renault-Dodge S56	Alexander AM	B25F	1987	Ex Western Scottish, 1995
	E646KYW	MCW MetroRider MF158/1	MCW	B30F	1987	Ex Stagecoach East London, 1995
	E648KYW	MCW MetroRider MF158/1	MCW	B30F	1987	Ex Stagecoach East London, 1995
	J3SLT	Mercedes-Benz 709D	Plaxton Beaver	B23F	1992	
	J4SLT	Mercedes-Benz 709D	Plaxton Beaver	B23F	1992	
	J8SLT	Dennis Dart 9.8SDL3017	Plaxton Pointer	B38F	1992	
	J9SLT	Dennis Dart 9.8SDL3017	Plaxton Pointer	B38F	1992	
	J10SLT	Mercedes-Benz 811D	Reeve Burgess Beaver	B31F	1991	Ex Mercedes demonstrator, 1993
	J988TVU	Mercedes-Benz 709D	Plaxton Beaver	B23F	1992	
	K1SLT	Mercedes-Benz 811D	Plaxton Beaver	B31F	1993	
	K2SLT	Mercedes-Benz 811D	Plaxton Beaver	B31F	1993	
	K3SLT	Mercedes-Benz 811D	Plaxton Beaver	B31F	1992	Ex Mercedes-Benz demonstrator, 1994
	L1SLT	Dennis Dart 9SDL3011	Plaxton Pointer	B35F	1993	
	L2SLT	Dennis Dart 9SDL3011	Plaxton Pointer	B35F	1993	
	L11SLT	Dennis Dart 9.8SDL3025	Plaxton Pointer	B38F	1993	
	J7SLT	Dennis Dart 9.8SDL30..	Plaxton Pointer	B38F	1996	
	J6SLT	Dennis Dart 9.8SDL30..	Plaxton Pointer	B40F	1996	

Previous Registrations:

49XBF	OSJ38X	J6SLT	N192BNB	J988TVU	J58MHS, J7SLT
J3SLT	J62MHF	J7SLT	From new	K3SLT	K455EDT, 30938(GBG), K455EDT
J4SLT	J61MHF	J10SLT	J470XHL		

Opposite: **Two vehicles with South Lancs-owned index plates are pictured here. The upper picture shows L2SLT, a Dennis Dart with Plaxton Pointer bodywork while the lower picture shows J4SLT. This is a Mercedes-Benz 709D with Plaxton Beaver bodywork. A recent addition to the operations around St Helens is a minibus network in Chester. A large number of Renault-Dodge S56 minibuses have been purchased to service this expansion and these carry a green and cream livery.**
Phillip Stephenson/Paul Wigan

TAYLORS

D & G Taylor, Monopol Buildings, Dennis Road, Widnes, Cheshire, WA8 0SN

TJI1695	Bristol LHL6L	Plaxton Elite III	C51F	1973	Ex Bassett, Tittensor, 1995
TJI1694	Leyland Leopard PSU5/4R	Duple Dominant	C57F	1974	Ex Bassett, Tittensor, 1995
TJI1693	AEC Reliance 6U3ZR	Duple Dominant	C53F	1975	Ex Ascot, Derby, 1995
TJI3373	Leyland Atlantean AN68A/1R	Northern Counties	H43/32F	1975	Ex Cardiff Bluebird, 1995
TJI3374	Leyland Fleetline FE30ALR	MCW	H45/32F	1976	Ex Jolly Roger, Haxby, 1995
TJI1691	AEC Reliance 6U3ZR	Duple Dominant	C53F	1977	Ex Aaron Travel, Rainhill, 1994
TJI3372	Leyland Leopard PSU3E/4R	Duple Dominant II	C47F	1978	Ex Brook, Oldham, 1995
TJI6325	Leyland Leopard PSU3E/4R	Duple Dominant II	C53F	1979	Ex Brook, Oldham, 1995
G421RCW	Volvo B58-61	Plaxton Supreme IV	C44FT	1979	Ex Redline Cs, Penwortham, 1994
TJI3369	Leyland Fleetline FE30AGR	Eastern Coach Works	H43/32F	1979	Ex Blue Bus, Derby, 1995
TJI6326	Leyland Fleetline FE30ALR	Northern Counties	H39/31F	1980	Ex West Riding, 1995
TJI1692	Leyland Leopard PSU3E/4R	Duple Dominant II	C49F	1980	Ex Dean, Batley, 1995
TJI1690	DAF MB200DKTL585	Plaxton Supreme V	C53F	1982	Ex Whittaker Travels, Preston, 1994

Livery: Blue and yellow

Previous Registrations:

G421RCW	GGD668T, BIB980	TJI3369	ULS656T
TJI1690	AVM21Y, VVU266, WEC349Y	TJI3372	PJG798S, 672RKJ, YKO79S
TJI1691	REK921R	TJI3373	KBU911P
TJI1692	EYH808V	TJI3374	KUC989P
TJI1693	KRG568P	TJI6325	AYF864T
TJI1694	VTB972M	TJI6326	LWT100V
TJI1695	XTF466L		

TOFTWOOD TRAVEL

F G Lovett, 11 Toftwood Avenue, Rainhill, Merseyside, L35 0PU

HSC166X	Leyland Cub CU435	Duple Dominant	B31F	1981	Ex Heaton Travel, Leigh, 1994
D794KWR	Freight Rover Sherpa	Dormobile	B20F	1987	Ex Nip-On, St Helens, 1993
E843JHG	Freight Rover Sherpa	Elme Orion	C16F	1988	Ex Neill, Arnold, 1990

Livery: Blue and white

TOWN FLIERS

J & S Pugh, 75 Eastham Crescent, Clock Face, St Helens, Merseyside, WA9 4ER

Depots : Burtonhead Road, St Helens

GTG634W	Leyland Leopard PSU3E/4R	Duple Dominant II Express	C53F	1980	Ex Cardiff Bus, 1994
ANK317X	Bedford YMQS	Lex Maxeta	B37F	1982	Ex Hutchison, Overtown, 1991
C51HDT	Dennis Domino SDA1202	Optare	B33F	1985	Ex Stevensons, 1992
C54HDT	Dennis Domino SDA1202	Optare	B33F	1985	Ex Stevensons, 1992
C802CBU	Renault-Dodge S56	Northern Counties	B18F	1986	Ex GM Buses, 1991
C806CBU	Renault-Dodge S56	Northern Counties	B18F	1986	Ex GM Buses, 1991
D844LND	Renault-Dodge S56	Northern Counties	B20F	1986	Ex GM Buses, 1991
D231TBW	Volkswagen LT55	Optare City Pacer	B25F	1987	Ex Lancaster, 1993
E748MSC	Mercedes-Benz 709D	Alexander AM	B25F	1988	Ex Carr, Whitburn, 1994
F202XBV	Freight Rover Sherpa	Carlyle Citybus 2	B20F	1989	Ex ABC Travel, Ainsdale, 1993
F795SFA	Renault-Dodge S56	PMT Bursley	B25F	1988	Ex Pride of the Road, Royston, 1993

Livery: Turquoise and white.

Taylors blue and yellow livery is worn in this picture of G421RCW, the only vehicle in the fleet not carrying a TJI mark. This Volvo B58 carries a Plaxton Supreme body and is probably the only G-reg B58 in existence, the mark having been issued on the vehicle's return from Northern Ireland.
Martin Grosberg

Town Fliers fleet is represented here by its newest and oldest vehicles. GTG634W is a Duple Dominant-bodied Leyland Leopard which came to the fleet in 1994 from Cardiff Bus. F795SFA is a Renault-Dodge S56 with PMT bodywork to their Bursley design and devoid of any destination equipment.
R L Wilson/ Paul Wigan

VILLAGE

C Hunter, 21 Church Road, Garston, Liverpool, L19 8EA

Depot: Evans Road, Speke, Liverpool

V1	GNF15V	Leyland Titan TNTL11/1RF	Park Royal	H47/26F	1979	Ex Universitybus, 1995
V2	CUL84V	Leyland Titan TNLXB/1RF	Park Royal	H44/26D	1980	Ex Kinch, Barrow-on-Soar, 1995
V3	JKB146L	Bedford YRQ	Duple Dominant	C41F	1973	Ex Trent, 1978
V4	RCH286R	Leyland Fleetline FE30AGR	Roe	H43/30F	1976	Ex Blue Bus, Derby, 1994
V5	OKY62R	AEC Reliance 6U3ZR	Plaxton Supreme III	C55F	1977	Ex National Travel East, 1981
V6	D927LYC	Mercedes-Benz L307D	Reeve Burgess	M12	1986	Ex Coombs, Weston-super-Mare, 1995
V7	CUL138V	Leyland Titan TNLXB/1RF	Park Royal	H44/26D	1980	Ex Kinch, Barrow-on-Soar, 1995
V8	XRR291S	Leyland Fleetline FE30AGR	Northern Counties	H43/30F	1978	Ex Blue Bus, Derby, 1994
V9	NOC598R	Leyland Fleetline FE30AGR	Park Royal	H43/33F	1976	Ex City Fleet, Bootle, 1993
V10	NOC489R	Leyland Fleetline FE30AGR	MCW	H43/33F	1977	Ex City Fleet, Bootle, 1993
V11	XRR295S	Leyland Fleetline FE30AGR	Northern Counties	H43/30F	1978	Ex Blue Bus, Derby, 1994
V12	XRR293S	Leyland Fleetline FE30AGR	Northern Counties	H43/30F	1978	Ex Blue Bus, Derby, 1994
V13	NOC726R	Leyland Fleetline FE30AGR	East Lancashire	H43/33F	1977	Ex Frontline, 1994
V14	XRR289S	Leyland Fleetline FE30AGR	Northern Counties	H43/30F	1978	Ex Blue Bus, Derby, 1994
V15	RCH288R	Leyland Fleetline FE30AGR	Roe	H43/30F	1976	Ex Blue Bus, Derby, 1994
V16	RCH283R	Leyland Fleetline FE30AGR	Roe	H43/30F	1976	Ex Blue Bus, Derby, 1994
V17	XRR294S	Leyland Fleetline FE30AGR	Northern Counties	H43/30F	1978	Ex Blue Bus, Derby, 1994
V18	KJD80P	Leyland Fleetline FE30ALR	Park Royal	H44/24D	1976	Ex Camms, Nottingham, 1994
V19	KWJ136P	Daimler Fleetline CRG6LX	Roe	H42/29D	1976	Ex Pennine Blue, 1994
V20	SDA658S	Leyland Fleetline FE30AGR	Park Royal	H43/33F	1978	Ex J C Coaches, Widnes, 1994
V21	RCH285R	Leyland Fleetline FE30AGR	Roe	H43/30F	1976	Ex Taylors, Widnes, 1994
V22	G490PNF	Mercedes-Benz 507D	Made-to-Measure	C20F	1989	Ex Woollon, Feltham, 1995
V23	XRR296S	Leyland Fleetline FE30AGR	Northern Counties	H43/30F	1978	Ex Blue Bus, Derby, 1994
V24	KON372P	Leyland Fleetline FE30ALR	MCW	H43/33F	1976	Ex Frontline, 1994
V25	NOC734R	Leyland Fleetline FE30AGR	East Lancashire	H43/33F	1977	Ex Ementon, Cranfield, 1994
V26	EDS537B	AEC Routemaster R2RH	Park Royal	H36/28R	1984	Ex Hallamshire Bus, Kilnhurst, 1994
V27	CUL165V	Leyland Titan TNLXB/1RF	Park Royal	H44/22D	1980	Ex Kinch, Barrow-on-Soar, 1995
V28	ASD25T	Leyland Fleetline FE30AGR	Alexander AL	H45/33F	1979	Ex Western Scottish, 1995
V29	ASD26T	Leyland Fleetline FE30AGR	Alexander AL	H45/33F	1979	Ex Western Scottish, 1995
V30	EGB80T	Leyland National 11351A/2R		B52F	1978	Ex A1 Service, 1995
V31	ASD27T	Leyland Fleetline FE30AGR	Alexander AL	H45/33F	1979	Ex A1 Service, 1995
V32	ASD29T	Leyland Fleetline FE30AGR	Alexander AL	H45/33F	1979	Ex A1 Service, 1995
V33	VCU402T	Leyland Fleetline FE30AGR	MCW	H43/32F	1979	Ex Western Scottish, 1995
V34	WDA914T	Leyland Fleetline FE30AGR	MCW	H43/33F	1978	Ex A1 Service, 1995
V35	SDA644S	Leyland Fleetline FE30AGR	Park Royal	H43/33F	1978	Ex A1 Service, 1995
V36	L5HMC	Leyland-DAF 400	Concept	M16	1993	Ex Williams, Halton, 1995
V37	CUL112V	Leyland Titan TNLXB/1RF	Park Royal	H44/26D	1980	Ex Kinch, Barrow-on-Soar, 1995
V38	CUL87V	Leyland Titan TNLXB/1RF	Park Royal	H44/22D	1980	Ex Kinch, Barrow-on-Soar, 1995
SKY1	RIB4310	Aüwaerter Neoplan N722/3	Plaxton Paramount 4000 II	CH53/18CT	1985	Ex Garnett, Tindale Crescent, 1995
G7	885NBH	DAF MB200DKTL600	Caetano Algarve	C53F	1984	Ex Knights, Ellesmere Port, 1989

Previous Registrations:

885NBH	A196FAY		JKB146L	TCH95L
EDS537B	630DYE		RIB4310	B170REF

Livery: Red and cream or grey (buses); gold, red, orange and yellow (coaches).

Opposite: **At one time Garston was just a village and this is from where the Village name has evolved. Mostly the fleet comprises Leyland Fleetline double deck buses with a variety of bodywork and these are to be found on various services in the area. Seen heading for Garston is V14, XRR289S, with Northern Counties bodywork. Following the sale of A1 to Western Scottish during 1995 several of that fleet were quickly sold, some having worked for Western while others were sold on without being used. Now with Village is V30, EGB80T, a Leyland National seen here in fleet livery and a vehicle which falls into the latter category.** *Malc McDonald/Richard Godfrey*

WALKERS

G E & M V Walker, Malvern House, Old Road, Anderton, Northwich, Cheshire, CW9 6AG

PRR106L	Bristol VRT/SL2/6LX	Eastern Coach Works	H39/31F	1972	Ex Crosville Wales, 1987
PRR108L	Bristol VRT/SL2/6LX	Eastern Coach Works	H39/31F	1972	Ex Crosville Wales, 1987
PRR110L	Bristol VRT/SL/26LX	Eastern Coach Works	H39/31F	1972	Ex Crosville Wales, 1989
RUK522L	Ford R226	Plaxton Elite III	C53F	1973	Ex National Travel Midlands, 1978
VTB591L	Ford R226	Duple Dominant	C53F	1973	Ex Cosgrove, Preston, 1976
XRR129M	Bristol VRT/SL2/6LX	Eastern Coach Works	H39/31F	1973	Ex East Midland, 1989
XRR132M	Bristol VRT/SL2/6LX	Eastern Coach Works	H39/31F	1973	Ex East Midland, 1989
XRR133M	Bristol VRT/SL2/6LX	Eastern Coach Works	H39/31F	1973	Ex East Midland, 1989
CJO468R	Bristol VRT/SL3/6LXB	Eastern Coach Works	H43/31F	1977	Ex Midland Red North, 1993
UUM500R	Ford R1114	Plaxton Supreme III	C53F	1977	
EYK512V	Volvo B58-61	Plaxton Supreme IV	C49FT	1980	Ex Robin Hood, Rudyard, 1989
296HFM	Volvo B58-61	Plaxton Supreme IV	C55F	1980	Ex Shearings, 1989
UTF119	Volvo B58-61	Plaxton Supreme IV	C57F	1980	Ex Wickson, Clayhanger, 1991
HOI7544	Volvo B58-56	Plaxton Supreme IV	C53F	1980	Ex Wickson, Clayhanger, 1991
152ENM	Volvo B58-61	Plaxton Supreme IV	C53F	1980	Ex Ingleby, Fulford, 1991
ASV237	Volvo B10M-61	Plaxton Supreme IV	C50F	1980	Ex Niddrie, Middlewich, 1989
ACA507A	Volvo B58-61	Plaxton Supreme IV	C53F	1981	Ex WHM, Brentwood, 1988
JHF826	Volvo B58-56	Plaxton Supreme IV	C53F	1981	Ex Woodstones, Kidderminster, 1988
ACA194A	Volvo B58-56	Plaxton Supreme IV	C53F	1981	Ex Cosgrove, Preston, 1989
505BRM	Volvo B10M-61	Duple Laser	C51F	1983	Ex Stewart, Dalmuir, 1985
A864KNA	Ford Transit 190	Dixon Lomas	M12	1983	
JHF824	Volvo B10M-61	Duple Laser	C51F	1984	
JHF825	Volvo B10M-61	Duple Laser	C51F	1984	Ex Park's, 1986
716GRM	Volvo B10M-61	Duple Laser	C51F	1984	
184XNO	Volvo B10M-61	Duple Laser	C51F	1984	Ex Globe, Barnsley, 1986
629LFM	Volvo B10M-61	Van Hool Alizée	C53F	1985	Ex Shearings, 1991
E701WNE	Mercedes-Benz 507D	Made-to-Measure	C16F	1988	
E702WNE	Mercedes-Benz 507D	Made-to-Measure	C16F	1988	
F433ENB	Mercedes-Benz 609D	Made-to-Measure	C21F	1988	
848AFM	Volvo B10M-61	Van Hool Alizée	C53F	1989	
H813JKB	Mercedes-Benz 609D	North West Coach Sales	C24F	1990	Ex van, 1994
H490BND	Mercedes-Benz 609D	Made-to-Measure	C24F	1990	Ex Roger Hill, Congleton, 1991

Previous Registrations:

152ENM	EYK513V	716GRM	B637LJU	HOI7544	JJU440V
184XNO	B359DWF	848AFM	F338SMD	JHF824	B636LJU
296HFM	JLS457V	ACA194A	BKD557X	JHF825	A731HFP
505BRM	XAO3Y	ACA507A	UNO823W	JHF826	KWJ864W
629LFM	B313UNB	ASV237	JSJ431W	UTF119	NGD941V

Livery: White and purple

The purple and white livery used by Walkers is seen on both double deck school buses and touring coaches. Above is ASV237, one of the early Volvo B10Ms with Plaxton Supreme bodywork, while below is XRR129M a Bristol VRT with Eastern Coach Works body. *Ralph Stevens/Bill Potter*

The blue and yellow livery applied by Warrington to its mini buses and early midibuses is giving way to the normal fleet livery as the operation competes with British Bus' town services. Still in MidiLines livery is 215, H843NOC, a Dennis Dart with Carlyle Dartline bodywork. *Tony Wilson*

Four East Lancashire-bodied Bristol RESLs are now the only full-size single-deck vehicles. When these were converted from dual-door 72, LED72P received high-back seating. The vehicle is seen parked at the bus station. *Richard Godfrey*

WARRINGTON

Warrington Borough Transport Ltd; Coachlines of Warrington Ltd
Wilderspool Causeway, Warrington, Cheshire, WA4 6PT

1	F101XEM	Dennis Dominator DDA1017	East Lancashire	H51/37F	1988
2	F102XEM	Dennis Dominator DDA1017	East Lancashire	H51/37F	1988
3	F103XEM	Dennis Dominator DDA1017	East Lancashire	H51/37F	1988
4	F104XEM	Dennis Dominator DDA1017	East Lancashire	H51/37F	1988

5-16

Leyland Atlantean AN68A/1R East Lancashire H45/31F 1978-80

5	XTB5T	8	XTB8T	11	XTB11T	13	GEK13V	15	GEK15V
6	XTB6T	9	XTB9T	12	GEK12V	14	GEK14V	16	GEK16V
7	XTB7T	10	XTB10T						

17-22

Leyland Atlantean AN68B/1R East Lancashire H45/31F 1980-81

| 17 | HED17V | 19 | MEK19W | 20 | MEK20W | 21 | MEK21W | 22 | MEK22W |
| 18 | MEK18W | | | | | | | | |

| 23 | MEK23W | Leyland Atlantean AN68C/1R | East Lancashire | H45/31F | 1981 |

24-28

Leyland Atlantean AN68C/1R East Lancashire H45/33F 1981

| 24 | OTB24W | 25 | OTB25W | 26 | OTB26W | 27 | OTB27W | 28 | OTB28W |

37	A207DTO	Leyland Olympian ONLXB/1R	East Lancashire	H45/31F	1984	Ex Derby, 1987
38	A206DTO	Leyland Olympian ONLXB/1R	East Lancashire	H45/31F	1984	Ex Derby, 1987
39	A209DTO	Leyland Olympian ONLXB/1R	East Lancashire	H45/31F	1984	Ex Derby, 1987
40	A210DTO	Leyland Olympian ONLXB/1R	East Lancashire	H45/31F	1984	Ex Derby, 1987

41-48

Dennis Dominator DDA156 East Lancashire H51/37F* 1982/83 *43-46 are type DDA159

| 41 | CLV41X | 43 | CLV43X | 46 | A746GFY | 47 | A747GFY | 48 | A748GFY |
| 42 | CLV42X | 45 | A745GFY | | | | | | |

67w	TWJ340Y	Dennis Falcon HC SDA410	East Lancashire	B52F	1983	Ex Ipswich, 1995
68w	TWJ341Y	Dennis Falcon HC SDA410	East Lancashire	B52F	1983	Ex Ipswich, 1995
69w	TWJ342Y	Dennis Falcon HC SDA410	East Lancashire	B52F	1983	Ex Ipswich, 1995
70	LED70P	Bristol RESL6G	East Lancashire	B41F	1976	
71	LED71P	Bristol RESL6G	East Lancashire	B44F	1976	
72	LED72P	Bristol RESL6G	East Lancashire	DP40F	1976	
73	LED73P	Bristol RESL6G	East Lancashire	B44F	1976	

74-83

Leyland Atlantean AN68A/1R East Lancashire H45/31F* 1977/78 *77 is H45/33F

| 74 | TTB74S | 76 | TTB76S | 78 | TTB78S | 80 | TTB80S | 82 | TTB82S |
| 75 | REK75R | 77 | REK77R | 79 | TTB79S | 81 | TTB81S | 83 | TTB83S |

84	CLV84X	Leyland Olympian ONLXB/2R	East Lancashire	H51/37F	1982
85	CLV85X	Leyland Olympian ONLXB/2R	East Lancashire	H51/37F	1982
86	A486HKB	Leyland Olympian ONLXB/2R	East Lancashire	H51/37F	1984
87	A487HKB	Leyland Olympian ONLXB/2R	East Lancashire	H51/37F	1984
91	B101SED	Leyland Olympian ONLXCT/2R	East Lancashire	DPH47/31F	1985
92	B102SED	Leyland Olympian ONLXCT/2R	East Lancashire	DPH47/31F	1985

95-99

Dennis Dominator DDA1017 East Lancashire H51/37F 1989

| 95 | F95STB | 96 | F96STB | 97 | F97STB | 98 | F98STB | 99 | F99STB |

Warrington double-deck 101, C101UBC, is a Dennis Dominator with East Lancashire bodywork and was new to Leicester from where it was acquired when only four years old. *Malc McDonald*

100	C100UBC	Dennis Dominator DDA1010	East Lancashire	H46/33F	1986	Ex Leicester, 1989
101	C101UBC	Dennis Dominator DDA1010	East Lancashire	H46/33F	1986	Ex Leicester, 1989
102	C102UBC	Dennis Dominator DDA1010	East Lancashire	H46/33F	1986	Ex Leicester, 1989
103	C103UBC	Dennis Dominator DDA1010	East Lancashire	H46/33F	1986	Ex Leicester, 1989
107	GHC519N	Leyland Atlantean AN68/1R	East Lancashire	H43/32F	1975	Ex Eastbourne, 1988
108	GHC522N	Leyland Atlantean AN68/1R	East Lancashire	H43/32F	1975	Ex Eastbourne, 1988
109	GHC524N	Leyland Atlantean AN68/1R	East Lancashire	H43/32F	1975	Ex Eastbourne, 1988
110	GHC525N	Leyland Atlantean AN68/1R	East Lancashire	H43/32F	1975	Ex Eastbourne, 1988
111	UFV113R	Leyland Atlantean AN68A/2R	East Lancashire	H50/36F	1976	Ex Preston Bus, 1990
112	UFV116R	Leyland Atlantean AN68A/2R	East Lancashire	H50/36F	1976	Ex Preston Bus, 1990
113	UFV117R	Leyland Atlantean AN68A/2R	East Lancashire	H50/36F	1976	Ex Preston Bus, 1990
114	UFV120R	Leyland Atlantean AN68A/2R	East Lancashire	H50/36F	1976	Ex Preston Bus, 1990
115	CBV118S	Leyland Atlantean AN68A/1R	East Lancashire	H45/31F	1978	Ex Blackburn, 1995
116	CBV123S	Leyland Atlantean AN68A/1R	East Lancashire	H45/31F	1978	Ex Blackburn, 1995
117	CBV119S	Leyland Atlantean AN68A/1R	East Lancashire	H45/31F	1978	Ex Blackburn, 1996
118	LFR125T	Leyland Atlantean AN68A/1R	East Lancashire	H45/31F	1979	Ex Blackburn, 1996
119	LFR126T	Leyland Atlantean AN68A/1R	East Lancashire	H45/31F	1979	Ex Blackburn, 1995
121	F121XEM	Dennis Dominator DDA1018	East Lancashire	DPH47/29F	1988	
122	F122XEM	Dennis Dominator DDA1018	East Lancashire	DPH47/29F	1988	
148	BED729C	Leyland PD2/40 Sp	East Lancashire	H34/30F	1965	
191	D767YCW	Renault-Dodge S56	Northern Counties	B22F	1987	Ex Preston Bus, 1995
192	E46GRN	Renault-Dodge S56	Northern Counties	B20F	1987	Ex Preston Bus, 1995
193	D757YCW	Renault-Dodge S56	Northern Counties	B22F	1987	Ex Preston Bus, 1995
194	D756YCW	Renault-Dodge S56	Northern Counties	B22F	1987	Ex Preston Bus, 1995
195	D753YCW	Renault-Dodge S56	Northern Counties	B22F	1987	Ex Preston Bus, 1995
196	D755YCW	Renault-Dodge S56	Northern Counties	B22F	1987	Ex Preston Bus, 1995

Page 95: Contrasting the body styles on two variants of the Dennis Dart are Warringtons 221, K221VTB bodied by Northern Counties and 238, M238YKD with a Plaxton Pointer body.

Opposite, top: Three Dennis Falcons were used on extended loan from Ipswich during 1995, all three are to be returned shortly. For their stay they were painted into Warrington's livery as illustrated by 68, TWJ341Y.

Opposite, bottom: Previously with Preston Bus, Warrington 196, D753YCW is one of six similar vehicles to arrive during 1995 as Warrington continued to react to the introduction of town services by North Western. This Northern Counties-bodied Renault-Dodge S56 is seen shortly after it received MiniLines livery. *All three by Richard Godfrey*

The Merseyside & Cheshire Bus Handbook

197	D700THF	Renault-Dodge S56	Alexander AM	B23F	1987	Ex Merseybus, 1994
198	D977TKC	Renault-Dodge S56	Alexander AM	B23F	1987	Ex Merseybus, 1994
199	D978TKC	Renault-Dodge S56	Alexander AM	B23F	1987	Ex Merseybus, 1994
200	D37NFU	Renault-Dodge S56	Alexander AM	B23F	1987	Ex Chester, 1994

201-206

Renault-Dodge S56 — Northern Counties — B22F* — 1987 — *201 is DP20F

201	D101TTJ	203	D103TTJ	204	D104TTJ	205	D105TTJ	206	D106TTJ
202	D102TTJ							

207-219

Dennis Dart 9SDL3003 — Carlyle Dartline — B35F* — 1991 — *212 is DP32F

207	H879LOX	210	H887LOX	213	H841NOC	216	H844NOC	218	H846NOC
208	H881LOX	211	H889LOX	214	H842NOC	217	H845NOC	219	H847NOC
209	H886LOX	212	H897LOX	215	H843NOC				

220	J10WBT	Dennis Dart 9SDL3003	Northern Counties Paladin	B33F	1991

221-225

Dennis Dart 9SDL3003 — Northern Counties Paladin — B33F — 1993

221	K221VTB	222	K222VTB	223	K223VTB	224	K224VTB	225	K225VTB

226-235

Dennis Dart 9SDL3034 — Northern Counties Paladin — B35F — 1993-94

226	L226SWM	228	L228SWM	230	L230SWM	232	L232SWM	234	L234SWM
227	L227SWM	229	L229SWM	231	L231SWM	233	L233SWM	235	L235SWM

236	M236YKD	Dennis Dart 9SDL3051	Plaxton Pointer	B35F	1995
237	M237YKD	Dennis Dart 9SDL3051	Plaxton Pointer	B35F	1995
238	M238YKD	Dennis Dart 9SDL3051	Plaxton Pointer	B35F	1995

239-243

Dennis Dart 9SDL3053 — Marshall C36 — B35F — 1995

239	M239YCM	240	M240YCM	241	M241YCM	242	M242YCM	243	M243YCM

244	M593HKH	Dennis Dart 9.8SDL3040	Plaxton Pointer	B40F	1994	Ex Plaxton demonstrator, 1995
245	M284HRH	Dennis Dart 9.8SDL3040	Plaxton Pointer	B40F	1994	Ex Plaxton demonstrator, 1995
246	M246YWM	Dennis Dart 9.8SDL3054	Plaxton Pointer	B40F	1995	
247	M247YLV	Dennis Dart 9.8SDL3054	Marshall C37	B40F	1995	
248	M248YLV	Dennis Dart 9.8SDL3054	Marshall C37	B40F	1995	

Coachlines

C1	G100TDJ	Volvo B10M-61	Van Hool Alizée	C49FT	1989
C2	J414AWF	Volvo B10M-60	Van Hool Alizée	C53F	1992
C3	J410AWF	Volvo B10M-60	Van Hool Alizée	C53F	1992

Livery: Red and white, yellow and blue (Coachlines)

The latest Darts for Warrington have been bodied by Marshall. Photographed on the Runcorn Busway is 242, M242YCM, one of the first midis to carry the Warrington red and white livery.
Philip Lamb

WHITEGATE TRAVEL

K L Prince, 15 Beauty Bank, Whitegate, Northwich, Cheshire, CW8 2BP

DLG899X	Mercedes-Benz L307D	Devon Conversions	M12	1982	Ex Simpson's, Keswick, 1992
D202FFX	Ford Transit	Carlyle	B16F	1986	Ex Castle, Weaverham, 1995
D203FFX	Ford Transit	Carlyle	B16F	1986	Ex Midland, 1995
D862OJA	Freight Rover Sherpa	Made-to-Measure	M16	1987	Ex Castle, Weaverham, 1995
E333HJM	Mercedes-Benz 307D	Economy	M12	1988	Ex Castle, Weaverham, 1995
E691UND	Freight Rover Sherpa	Made-to-Measure	M16	1987	Ex Castle, Weaverham, 1995
F504COM	Freight Rover Sherpa	Freight Rover	M16	1988	Ex Widnes Mini Coaches, 1993
CHR998	Leyland-DAF 400	Crystals	M14	1990	Ex van, 1993
J708MSD	Leyland-DAF 400	AMC	M16	1991	Ex Castle, Weaverham, 1995
M423TJO	LDV 200	LDV	M12	1994	

Livery: Yellow & white

Minibuses of Whitegate Travel are housed in this attractive hamlet a few kilometres from Northwich. A variety of minibuses are used mostly on school services and private hire. The latest addition to the fleet is M423TJO, seen here at base. *Bill Potter*

WINGATES TOURS

M & P Bold, 43 Spencers Lane, Melling, Liverpool, L31 1HB

MWW561P	Leyland Leopard PSU3C/4R	Plaxton Supreme III Express	C49F	1976	Ex Aintree Coachlines, 1990
YBN631V	Leyland Leopard PSU3E/4R	Plaxton Supreme IV Express	C51F	1979	Ex Chester, 1992
SCH153X	Leyland Leopard PSU3F/4R	Willowbrook 003	C49F	1982	Ex Trent Buses, 1993
WSU891	Volvo B10M-61	Caetano Algarve	C49FT	1986	Ex Goodwin, Stockport, 1989
C777PNU	Volvo B10M-61	Plaxton Paramount 3500 II	C53F	1986	Ex Blue Bus, Derby, 1995
TOH2S	Volvo B10M-61	Plaxton Paramount 3500 III	C51F	1987	Ex Park's, 1989
D558FFL	Volvo B10M-61	Plaxton Paramount 3500 III	C49FT	1987	Ex Turners, Bristol, 1996
D559FFL	Volvo B10M-61	Plaxton Paramount 3500 III	C49FT	1987	Ex Turners, Bristol, 1996
E838EUT	Volvo B10M-61	Duple 340	C53F	1987	Ex Tain Coaches, 1992
E148AJC	Freight Rover Sherpa	Carlyle Citybus 2	B20F	1988	Ex Crosville Wales, 1992
F564ESU	Volvo B10M-61	Ikarus Blue Danube	C53F	1988	Ex Glen Coaches, Port Glasgow, 1994
F107SSE	Volvo B10M-61	Ikarus Blue Danube	C53F	1989	Ex Hardings, Hyton, 1996
F551GHS	Volvo B10M-61	Ikarus Blue Danube	C53F	1988	Ex Glen Coaches, Port Glasgow, 1994
G563VHY	Volvo B10M-60	Plaxton Expressliner	C46FT	1989	Ex Wessex, 1995
K423THG	Mercedes-Benz 711D	PCW Coachworks	B18F	1993	
K427THG	Mercedes-Benz 709D	PCW Coachworks	B18F	1993	

Previous Registrations:

D558FFL	D813SGB, ESU913	TOH2S	D816SGB
D559FFL	D802SGB, ESU920	WSU891	C691KDS

Livery: Pink and white.

Wingates operate two Mercedes-Benz 709s with PCW Coachwork conversions. Pictured passing through St Georges Place in Liverpool is K423THG. *Richard Godfrey*

Index

The latest arrival with ABC Travel is this DAF SB220 with Northern Counties Paladin bodywork. N600ABC was photographed in Clitheroe with the destination blind set for a service 280 journey to Preston. *Paul Wigan*

AHW204V	Happy Al's	B65WUL	MTL	B148TRN	North Western	B530AYA	Grand Edwardian
AHW205V	Happy Al's	B66WUL	MTL	B148WUL	MTL	B693BPU	MTL
AIA1120	A1A Travel	B67WUL	MTL	B149TRN	North Western	B694BPU	MTL
AIA5505	A1A Travel	B75WUL	MTL	B149WUL	MTL	B784RNA	Ladyline
AIA9000	A1A Travel	B76WUL	MTL	B150TRN	North Western	B807OVT	Nova Scotia
AIA9030	A1A Travel	B77WUL	MTL	B150WUL	MTL	B834CDM	Bostock's
AKU161T	C M T	B78WUL	MTL	B151TRN	North Western	B847AFM	Bostock's
ALG130S	Bostock's	B79WUL	MTL	B151WUL	MTL	B854OSB	Bennett's
ALG163J	Lofty's	B80WUL	MTL	B153TRN	North Western	B926KWM	MTL
ALM23B	MTL	B81WUL	MTL	B153WUL	MTL	B960WRN	North Western
ALM41B	MTL	B82WUL	MTL	B154TRN	North Western	B962WRN	North Western
ALM971B	MTL	B83WUL	MTL	B155TRN	North Western	B963WRN	North Western
ALM979B	MTL	B87CDS	Ladyline	B156WUL	MTL	B964WRN	North Western
ALS645V	Happy Al's	B101SED	Warrington	B157WUL	MTL	B965WRN	North Western
ANC578A	Avon Buses	B102SED	Warrington	B158WUL	MTL	B966WRN	North Western
ANE2T	Aintree Coachlines	B107UFV	Chester	B159WUL	MTL	B967WRN	North Western
ANK317X	Town Flyers	B108UFV	Chester	B160WUL	MTL	B968WRN	North Western
ARN891Y	MTL	B111WUL	MTL	B161WUL	MTL	B969WRN	North Western
ARN893Y	MTL	B113WUL	MTL	B163PRK	Selwyns	BCA126W	Bostock's
ARN894Y	MTL	B114WUL	MTL	B163WUL	MTL	BCB613V	Chester
ASD25T	Village	B115WUL	MTL	B201EFM	Chester	BCB617V	Merseyline
ASD26T	Village	B117WUL	MTL	B202EFM	Chester	BCB618V	Merseyline
ASD27T	Village	B118WUL	MTL	B203EFM	Chester	BCD803L	C M T
ASD29T	Village	B119WUL	MTL	B204EFM	Chester	BCW823V	MTL
ASV237	Walkers	B120WUL	MTL	B231RRU	Arrowbrooke	BCW824V	MTL
AYR303T	C M T	B122NKB	Happy Al's	B234WUL	MTL	BED729C	Warrington
AYR321T	C M T	B131SED	Halton	B250WUL	MTL	BFM293L	Aintree Coachlines
B1BUS	Jim Stones	B132SED	Halton	B262VDB	Anthony's Travel	BFV900R	Nip-On
B43UCK	South Lancs	B141WUL	MTL	B277WUL	MTL	BHY999V	MTL
B58WUL	MTL	B142WUL	MTL	B284WUL	MTL	BNC935T	MTL
B59WUL	MTL	B143WUL	MTL	B287WUL	MTL	BNE733N	Avon Buses
B60WUL	MTL	B145WUL	MTL	B292WUL	MTL	BOK26V	North Western
B61WUL	MTL	B146WUL	MTL	B319RJF	Huxley	BOK32V	North Western
B63WUL	MTL	B147WUL	MTL	B483UNB	MTL	BOK33V	North Western

Reg	Operator	Reg	Operator	Reg	Operator	Reg	Operator
BOK34V	North Western	C334BUV	MTL	CUL70V	MTL	CUL207V	MTL
BOK36V	North Western	C355BUV	MTL	CUL71V	Aintree Coachlines	CUL210V	MTL
BOK40V	North Western	C365BUV	MTL	CUL72V	Aintree Coachlines	CUL211V	MTL
BOK50V	North Western	C369BUV	MTL	CUL73V	MTL	CUL213V	MTL
BOK51V	North Western	C375CAS	MTL	CUL74V	Aintree Coachlines	CUL217V	MTL
BOK52V	North Western	C376CAS	MTL	CUL77V	MTL	CUL218V	MTL
BOK53V	North Western	C377CAS	MTL	CUL82V	MTL	CUL219V	MTL
BOK54V	North Western	C378CAS	Chester	CUL84V	Village	CUL220V	MTL
BOK65V	North Western	C379CAS	Chester	CUL87V	Village	CUV136C	MTL
BOK67V	North Western	C380CAS	Chester	CUL91V	Avon Buses	CUV153C	MTL
BOK77V	North Western	C385BUV	MTL	CUL93V	Aintree Coachlines	CUV186C	MTL
BOK78V	North Western	C390BUV	MTL	CUL96V	Avon Buses	CUV282C	MTL
BOK79V	North Western	C392BUV	MTL	CUL97V	MTL	CUV284C	MTL
BOK90V	North Western	C393BUV	MTL	CUL101V	MTL	CUV295C	MTL
BPL476T	North Western	C394BUV	MTL	CUL102V	MTL	CUV296C	MTL
BPL477T	C M T	C395BUV	MTL	CUL103V	MTL	CUV310C	MTL
BPL486T	North Western	C396BUV	MTL	CUL104V	MTL	CWX657T	City Bus
BTB22T	Halton	C397BUV	MTL	CUL106V	MTL	D21RPP	Nova Scotia
BTB23T	Halton	C403BUV	MTL	CUL107V	MTL	D25RPP	Nova Scotia
BTB24T	Halton	C414BUV	MTL	CUL108V	MTL	D29PVS	Mercury
BTU374S	North Western	C531BFB	David Tanner	CUL109V	MTL	D32MWN	City Bus
BTW359V	North Western	C535BHY	David Tanner	CUL111V	MTL	D37NFU	Warrington
BTW367V	North Western	C542BHY	David Tanner	CUL112V	Village	D51RLG	Lofty's
BTW379V	North Western	C553BHY	MTL	CUL115V	MTL	D53STJ	A2B Travel
BTW402V	North Western	C567BHY	David Tanner	CUL116V	MTL	D71WTO	J C Mini
BTW406V	North Western	C652DNE	Anthony's Travel	CUL117V	MTL	D72WTO	J C Mini
BTW412V	North Western	C777PNU	Wingates	CUL118V	MTL	D101TTJ	Warrington
BTW413V	North Western	C802CBU	Town Flyers	CUL121V	MTL	D102TTJ	Warrington
BTW427V	North Western	C806CBU	Town Flyers	CUL122V	MTL	D103TTJ	Warrington
BTW430V	North Western	C854EML	Lofty's	CUL123V	MTL	D104TTJ	Warrington
BTW432V	North Western	C974PFS	Happy Al's	CUL124V	MTL	D105TTJ	Warrington
BTW437V	North Western	CBV15S	Happy Al's	CUL125V	MTL	D106TTJ	Warrington
BUS1N	Jim Stones	CBV118S	Warrington	CUL127V	MTL	D110OWG	South Lancs
BUS1T	Jim Stones	CBV119S	Warrington	CUL128V	MTL	D119WCC	Acorn Travel
BVP811V	North Western	CBV123S	Warrington	CUL129V	MTL	D120WCC	Huxley
BYW387V	MTL	CBV766S	North Western	CUL132V	MTL	D122OWG	South Lancs
BYX98V	MTL	CBV767S	North Western	CUL134V	MTL	D130NON	MTL
BYX101V	MTL	CBV773S	North Western	CUL135V	MTL	D139LTA	Mercury
BYX103V	MTL	CBV774S	North Western	CUL136V	MTL	D154THG	South Lancs
BYX114V	MTL	CBV786S	North Western	CUL138V	Village	D163WTV	North Western
BYX115V	MTL	CBV787S	North Western	CUL141V	MTL	D164UTO	North Western
BYX117V	MTL	CBV791S	North Western	CUL144V	MTL	D202FFX	Whitegate
BYX118V	MTL	CBV792S	North Western	CUL145V	MTL	D203FFX	Whitegate
BYX124V	MTL	CBV793S	North Western	CUL147V	MTL	D211SKD	North Western
BYX126V	MTL	CBV794S	North Western	CUL148V	MTL	D212SKD	North Western
BYX130V	MTL	CBV796S	North Western	CUL151V	MTL	D213SKD	North Western
BYX133V	MTL	CCY817V	North Western	CUL154V	MTL	D214SKD	North Western
BYX139V	MTL	CEO723W	MTL	CUL155V	MTL	D216SKD	North Western
BYX145V	MTL	CFM87S	Chester	CUL156V	MTL	D217SKD	North Western
BYX148T	MTL	CFM350S	North Western	CUL158V	MTL	D219SKD	North Western
BYX160T	MTL	CFM351S	North Western	CUL159V	MTL	D221SKD	North Western
BYX161T	MTL	CHR998	Whitegate	CUL160V	MTL	D223GLJ	Mercury
BYX181T	MTL	CJO468R	Walkers	CUL161V	MTL	D223NCS	South Lancs
BYX189T	MTL	CKB165X	MTL	CUL165V	Village	D225NCS	South Lancs
BYX194T	MTL	CKB166X	MTL	CUL166V	MTL	D225SKD	North Western
BYX199T	MTL	CKB167X	MTL	CUL170V	MTL	D226NCS	South Lancs
BYX231V	MTL	CKB168X	MTL	CUL171V	MTL	D227NCS	South Lancs
BYX243V	MTL	CKB169X	MTL	CUL174V	MTL	D228NCS	South Lancs
BYX294V	MTL	CKB170X	MTL	CUL177V	MTL	D229GLJ	MTL
C49OCM	Halton	CKC623X	MTL	CUL178V	MTL	D230NCS	South Lancs
C51HDT	Town Flyers	CKC624X	MTL	CUL182V	MTL	D231TBW	Town Flyers
C54HDT	Town Flyers	CKC626X	MTL	CUL184V	MTL	D233NCS	South Lancs
C54WBF	MTL	CKC928X	Halton	CUL187V	MTL	D236NCS	South Lancs
C100UBC	Warrington	CKC929X	Halton	CUL188V	MTL	D240NCS	South Lancs
C101UBC	Warrington	CLV41X	Warrington	CUL192V	MTL	D242NCS	South Lancs
C102UBC	Warrington	CLV42X	Warrington	CUL194V	MTL	D245NCS	South Lancs
C103UBC	Warrington	CLV43X	Warrington	CUL196V	MTL	D249NCS	South Lancs
C227EME	Hardings	CLV84X	Warrington	CUL199V	MTL	D250NCS	South Lancs
C325BUV	MTL	CLV85X	Warrington	CUL200V	Village	D255NCS	South Lancs
C329BUV	MTL	CNB253M	C M T	CUL201V	MTL	D257NCS	South Lancs
C330BUV	MTL	CRE791M	Roger Hill	CUL203V	MTL	D258NCS	South Lancs
C331BUV	MTL	CRY33T	Avon Buses	CUL204V	MTL	D259NCS	South Lancs
C333BUV	MTL	CUL68V	Avon Buses	CUL205V	MTL	D260NCS	South Lancs

Reg	Operator	Reg	Operator	Reg	Operator	Reg	Operator
D303SDS	South Lancs	D893DSF	Nip-On	E40YMB	Chester	E691UND	Whitegate
D305SDS	South Lancs	D920MVU	Mercury	E41PJV	Chester	E701WNE	Walkers
D390SGS	City Bus	D923PRJ	Arrowbrooke	E41YMB	Chester	E702WNE	Walkers
D403NNA	North Western	D927LYC	Village	E42PJV	Chester	E706WNE	Nova Scotia
D404NNA	North Western	D962DWD	Anthony's Travel	E43SBO	Chester	E748MSC	Town Flyers
D405NNA	North Western	D977TKC	Warrington	E46GRN	Warrington	E759HJF	Ogden's
D406NNA	North Western	D978TKC	Warrington	E49WEM	Halton	E763CNL	J C Mini
D408NNA	North Western	DAE510W	MTL	E56MMT	A2B Travel	E790SJA	Nova Scotia
D409NNA	North Western	DAE511W	MTL	E75PUH	Matthews	E801UDT	J C Mini
D410NNA	North Western	DAE512W	MTL	E126LAD	Chester	E803UDT	J C Mini
D411NNA	North Western	DAE513W	MTL	E134XCA	Chester	E806UDT	J C Mini
D412FEH	MTL	DAE514W	MTL	E135XCA	Chester	E807UDT	J C Mini
D413NNA	North Western	DBV3W	Chester	E136XCA	Chester	E809UDT	J C Mini
D416NNA	North Western	DBV4W	Chester	E137RAX	Acorn Travel	E810UDT	J C Mini
D417NNA	North Western	DBV133Y	North Western	E137XCA	Chester	E811JSX	Bennett's
D418NNA	North Western	DBV135Y	North Western	E146RNY	A1A Travel	E815XKD	Hardings
D419NNA	North Western	DBV136Y	North Western	E148AJC	Wingates	E835EUT	A2B Travel
D421NNA	North Western	DBV836W	MTL	E150AJC	Acorn Travel	E838EUT	Wingates
D424NNA	North Western	DBV840W	MTL	E201WBG	MTL	E843JHG	Toftwood
D425NNA	North Western	DBV845W	North Western	E202WBG	MTL	E889CDS	Chester
D426NNA	North Western	DCA522X	Bostock's	E203WBG	MTL	E898SDW	Dobson's
D427NNA	North Western	DEM758Y	MTL	E204WBG	MTL	E909EAY	Ogden's
D428NNA	North Western	DEM759Y	MTL	E205WBG	MTL	E913KYR	MTL
D431NNA	North Western	DEM760Y	MTL	E206WBG	MTL	E916KYR	MTL
D433NNA	North Western	DEM761Y	MTL	E207WBG	MTL	E925CDS	Chester
D435NNA	North Western	DEM762Y	MTL	E208WBG	MTL	E926KYR	MTL
D437NNA	North Western	DEM763Y	MTL	E209WBG	MTL	E928KYR	MTL
D437TMB	Bostock's	DEM773Y	MTL	E210WBG	MTL	E935CDS	Chester
D438TMB	Bostock's	DEM774Y	MTL	E212WBG	MTL	E938CDS	Chester
D439NNA	North Western	DEM775Y	MTL	E213WBG	MTL	E941CDS	Chester
D442NNA	North Western	DEM776Y	MTL	E214WBG	MTL	E968SVP	Matthews
D445NNA	North Western	DEM777Y	MTL	E215WBG	MTL	EDC406V	Meredith
D446NNA	North Western	DEM778Y	MTL	E216WBG	MTL	EDS537B	Village
D558FFL	Wingates	DEM779Y	MTL	E217WBG	MTL	EGB80T	Village
D559FFL	Wingates	DEM780Y	MTL	E218WBG	MTL	EGF285B	Acorn Travel
D589MVR	ABC Travel	DEM781Y	MTL	E219WBG	MTL	EKA156Y	MTL
D620YCX	Selwyns	DEM782Y	MTL	E220WBG	MTL	EKA157Y	MTL
D631RTM	A2B Travel	DEM783Y	MTL	E221WBG	MTL	EKA171Y	MTL
D670SEM	Arrowbrooke	DEM784Y	MTL	E222WBG	MTL	EKA215Y	MTL
D672SEM	Arrowbrooke	DEM785Y	MTL	E223WBG	MTL	EKA217Y	MTL
D679SEM	MTL	DEM786Y	MTL	E224BVR	North Western	EKA219Y	MTL
D680SEM	MTL	DEM787Y	MTL	E224WBG	MTL	EKA220Y	MTL
D682SEM	MTL	DEM788Y	MTL	E225BVR	North Western	EMB360S	North Western
D683SEM	MTL	DEM789Y	MTL	E225WBG	MTL	EMB366S	North Western
D684SEM	MTL	DEM790Y	MTL	E226WBG	MTL	EMB367S	North Western
D685SEM	MTL	DEM791Y	MTL	E227WBG	MTL	EMB370S	City Bus
D687SEM	MTL	DFR966W	Bostock's	E228WBG	MTL	EMB643S	North Western
D688SEM	MTL	DKC300L	MTL	E229WBG	MTL	EON823V	North Western
D689SEM	MTL	DKC301L	MTL	E230WBG	MTL	EON830V	City Bus
D690SEM	MTL	DKC305L	MTL	E270BRG	Mercury	EPD534V	Nova Scotia
D691SEM	MTL	DKC306L	MTL	E280XCA	Bostock's	EPH230V	North Western
D700THF	Warrington	DKC307L	MTL	E281XCA	Bostock's	ERP552T	C M T
D711SKB	Halton	DKC308L	MTL	E332LHG	J C Mini	ERP553T	C M T
D732JUB	A2B Travel	DKC309L	MTL	E333HJM	Whitegate	ERP555T	C M T
D753YCW	Warrington	DKC310L	MTL	E351SWY	Merseyside	ESK879	Huxley
D755YCW	Warrington	DKC311L	MTL	E386CNE	North Western	ESK882	Huxley
D756YCW	Warrington	DKC313L	MTL	E427ATT	Selwyns	EWM630Y	Halton
D757YCW	Warrington	DKC329L	MTL	E444MMM	Happy Al's	EYE231V	MTL
D767YCW	Warrington	DKC342L	MTL	E452SON	MTL	EYE232V	MTL
D794KWR	Toftwood	DKC360L	MTL	E453SON	MTL	EYE234V	MTL
D798KWR	Bennett's	DKC361L	MTL	E455SON	MTL	EYE239V	MTL
D804MNY	Nip-On	DKC369L	MTL	E457TYG	Merseyside	EYE241V	MTL
D81BCK	Mercury	DKC378L	MTL	E463ANC	Arrowbrooke	EYE242V	MTL
D844LND	Town Flyers	DKC391L	MTL	E510CHS	Selwyns	EYE243V	MTL
D845RHS	Selwyns	DKC392L	MTL	E525DCU	Nova Scotia	EYE245V	MTL
D846CRY	J C Mini	DLG899X	Whitegate	E576UNE	Matthews	EYE247V	MTL
D846RHS	Selwyns	DOI9172	Ogden's	E641VFY	Halton	EYE249V	MTL
D847CRY	J C Mini	DWH682W	Chester	E642VFY	Halton	EYE322V	MTL
D849LND	South Lancs	DWH685W	Merseyline	E646KYW	South Lancs	EYE328V	MTL
D850CRY	J C Mini	E25BTU	Chester	E648KYW	South Lancs	EYE341V	MTL
D852CRY	J C Mini	E38YFM	Chester	E658OCW	Anthony's Travel	EYK512V	Walkers
D862OJA	Whitegate	E39YMB	Chester	E685UVR	MTL	EYL318V	Ladyline
D868MDB	Nip-On	E40PJV	Chester	E688WNE	Nova Scotia	EYY327B	MTL

B500MPY has recently gained index mark B1BUS now that the DVLA has released the marks B1-B20 to the public. This design seen in the joint DAB/Eastern Coach Works product is similar to the DAB body style common on Leyland products, including the Leopard, in Denmark. *Paul Wigan*

F22TMP	Jim Stones	F237YTJ	MTL	F360MUT	Selwyns	F504COM	Whitegate
F32ALV	MTL	F238YTJ	MTL	F363CHE	Hardings	F518HUS	Nova Scotia
F48ALS	Happy Al's	F239YTJ	MTL	F368CHE	Arrowbrooke	F520AEM	Halton
F68GTU	MTL	F240YTJ	MTL	F373HMB	MTL	F521AEM	Halton
F73UJX	Aintree Coachlines	F241YTJ	MTL	F379CHE	Hardings	F551GHS	Wingates
F81STB	Halton	F242YTJ	MTL	F388CKU	Mercury	F564ESU	Wingates
F95STB	Warrington	F243YTJ	MTL	F391DOA	J C Mini	F600GET	Hardings
F96STB	Warrington	F244YTJ	MTL	F399KTU	Selwyns	F624XDA	Acorn Travel
F97STB	Warrington	F245YTJ	MTL	F421GWG	MTL	F630BKD	North Western
F98STB	Warrington	F246YTJ	MTL	F422GWG	MTL	F631BKD	North Western
F99STB	Warrington	F247YTJ	MTL	F423GWG	MTL	F632BKD	North Western
F101XEM	Warrington	F248YTJ	MTL	F424GWG	MTL	F633BKD	North Western
F102XEM	Warrington	F249HDB	J C Mini	F425GWG	MTL	F634BKD	North Western
F103XEM	Warrington	F249YTJ	MTL	F426GWG	MTL	F635BKD	North Western
F104XEM	Warrington	F250YTJ	MTL	F427GWG	MTL	F636BKD	North Western
F107SSE	Wingates	F251YTJ	MTL	F428GWG	MTL	F637BKD	North Western
F112YVP	Avon Buses	F252YTJ	MTL	F429GWG	MTL	F638BKD	North Western
F121XEM	Warrington	F253YTJ	MTL	F430BFY	A1A Travel	F639BKD	North Western
F122XEM	Warrington	F254YTJ	MTL	F433ENB	Walkers	F660OHD	Ogden's
F130KAO	A2B Travel	F255YTJ	MTL	F438AKB	MTL	F687YWM	Halton
F133KAO	A2B Travel	F256YTJ	MTL	F439AKB	MTL	F724JTU	Selwyns
F136KAO	A2B Travel	F257YTJ	MTL	F440AKB	MTL	F777GNA	ABC Travel
F182JFW	J C Mini	F258YTJ	MTL	F441AKB	MTL	F795SFA	Town Flyers
F199BCW	Dobson's	F259YTJ	MTL	F442AKB	MTL	F801YLV	MTL
F202XBV	Town Flyers	F260YTJ	MTL	F442DKM	J C Mini	F802YLV	MTL
F203XBV	ABC Travel	F261YTJ	MTL	F447DUG	Bostock's	F803YLV	MTL
F209JMB	Chester	F262YTJ	MTL	F448DUG	Bostock's	F804YLV	MTL
F210JMB	Chester	F263YTJ	MTL	F448LBA	Nova Scotia	F805YLV	MTL
F212AKG	A1A Travel	F264YTJ	MTL	F452XON	A1A Travel	F806YLV	MTL
F215BJX	Ogden's	F265YTJ	MTL	F455BKF	MTL	F807YLV	MTL
F223AKG	A2B Travel	F266YTJ	MTL	F456BKF	MTL	F808YLV	MTL
F231YTJ	MTL	F267YTJ	MTL	F457BKF	MTL	F809YLV	MTL
F232YTJ	MTL	F268YTJ	MTL	F458BKF	MTL	F810YLV	MTL
F233YTJ	MTL	F269YTJ	MTL	F459BKF	MTL	F811YLV	MTL
F234YTJ	MTL	F270YTJ	MTL	F481KFM	Bostock's	F812YLV	MTL
F235YTJ	MTL	F352DVR	ABC Travel	F481SDU	Nova Scotia	F813YLV	MTL
F236YTJ	MTL	F354DVR	ABC Travel	F482KFM	Bostock's	F814YLV	MTL

MTL 6301, L301TEM, is one of the three Volvo B10Bs in the MTL fleet with Alexander Strider bodywork and is seen with Merseyrider names en route for Halewood. *Roy Marshall*

F815YLV	MTL	FBV508W	North Western	G110KUB	MTL	G438GJC	Roger Hill
F816YLV	MTL	FBV509W	North Western	G110TND	North Western	G473DHF	Halton
F817YLV	MTL	FBV510W	North Western	G111KUB	MTL	G474DHF	Halton
F818YLV	MTL	FBV511W	North Western	G112KUB	MTL	G490PNF	Village
F819RJF	Hardings	FBV512W	North Western	G112TND	North Western	G563VHY	Wingates
F819YLV	MTL	FBV513W	North Western	G113KUB	MTL	G569BHP	J C Mini
F820YLV	MTL	FBV514W	North Western	G114KUB	MTL	G602SJA	Dobson's
F821YLV	MTL	FBV515W	North Western	G115KUB	MTL	G610CFA	North Western
F822YLV	MTL	FBX562W	Ladyline	G116KUB	MTL	G611CFA	North Western
F823YLV	MTL	FCA7X	North Western	G117KUB	MTL	G612CFA	North Western
F824YLV	MTL	FCA10X	North Western	G118KUB	MTL	G626EKA	North Western
F825YLV	MTL	FIL5123	Aintree Coachlines	G118TND	North Western	G627EKA	North Western
F867TNH	Lofty's	FIL7290	Acorn Travel	G119TND	North Western	G628EKA	North Western
F869TNH	Lofty's	FTU382T	North Western	G120KUB	MTL	G629EKA	North Western
F882VSJ	Chester	FTU386T	North Western	G121KUB	MTL	G640CHF	North Western
F894XOE	Acorn Travel	FTU391T	North Western	G123TJA	North Western	G641CHF	North Western
F895BKF	Halton	FUJ937V	Huxley	G124TJA	North Western	G642CHF	North Western
F915KCA	Bostock's	FV4548	Grand Edwardian	G125TJA	North Western	G643CHF	North Western
FBV486W	North Western	FVM741V	Dobson's	G132ORP	Anthony's Travel	G644EVN	North Western
FBV487W	North Western	G27XBK	Lofty's	G146TGX	J C Mini	G647EKA	North Western
FBV488W	North Western	G34HKY	North Western	G147TGX	J C Mini	G648EKA	North Western
FBV489W	North Western	G35HKY	North Western	G148TGX	J C Mini	G649EKA	North Western
FBV490W	North Western	G36HKY	North Western	G214AHP	Mercury	G650EKA	North Western
FBV491W	North Western	G37HKY	North Western	G220EOA	Matthews	G651EKA	North Western
FBV492W	North Western	G38HKY	North Western	G221DKA	Halton	G652EKA	North Western
FBV493W	North Western	G41HKY	North Western	G222DKA	Halton	G653EKA	North Western
FBV494W	North Western	G100TDJ	Warrington	G228HCP	Ogden's	G655EVN	Arrowbrooke
FBV495W	North Western	G100TND	North Western	G260EHD	MTL	G659DTJ	North Western
FBV496W	North Western	G102TND	North Western	G381EKA	North Western	G660DTJ	North Western
FBV497W	North Western	G103TND	North Western	G382EKA	North Western	G661DTJ	North Western
FBV498W	North Western	G104TND	North Western	G383EKA	North Western	G663FKA	North Western
FBV499W	North Western	G105TND	North Western	G384EKA	North Western	G664FKA	North Western
FBV500W	North Western	G106TND	North Western	G385EKA	North Western	G665FKA	North Western
FBV503W	North Western	G107TND	North Western	G386EKA	North Western	G667FKA	North Western
FBV504W	North Western	G108KUB	MTL	G387EKA	North Western	G711LKW	North Western
FBV505W	North Western	G108TND	North Western	G388EKA	North Western	G712VRY	Hardings
FBV506W	North Western	G109KUB	MTL	G391ORR	J C Mini	G714LKW	North Western
FBV507W	North Western	G109TND	North Western	G421RCW	Taylors	G771FJC	Mercury

Reg	Operator	Reg	Operator	Reg	Operator	Reg	Operator
G774FJC	Mercury	GKA529M	MTL	H112OON	Selwyns	HPV849	Hardings
G801OVA	MTL	GKA535M	MTL	H113OON	Selwyns	HSB739Y	Nip-On
G802OVA	MTL	GMB375T	North Western	H129CDB	North Western	HSB740Y	Nip-On
G803EKA	Halton	GMB379T	North Western	H130CDB	North Western	HSC109T	C M T
G803OVA	MTL	GMB380T	North Western	H146EKM	Anthony's Travel	HSC110T	C M T
G804OVA	MTL	GMB384T	North Western	H184CNS	Lofty's	HSC112T	C M T
G900CRW	Arrowbrooke	GMB385T	North Western	H233BBA	Halton Mini	HSC113T	C M T
G922EKF	MTL	GMB386T	North Western	H392KPY	J C Mini	HSC166X	Toftwood
G950RFL	MTL	GMB392T	North Western	H399HTJ	Hardings	HSJ61V	Aintree Coachlines
G951RFL	MTL	GMB657T	North Western	H404BVR	North Western	HTJ626P	MTL
G952RFL	MTL	GMB663T	North Western	H407BVR	North Western	HTJ627P	MTL
G953RFL	MTL	GMB666T	North Western	H434DVM	Arrowbrooke	HTJ628P	MTL
G956SMB	Bostock's	GMB667T	North Western	H451AGB	J C Mini	HTJ630P	MTL
G966SND	Halton Mini	GMB668T	North Western	H466HBA	A2B Travel	HTJ631P	MTL
G995LAH	Nova Scotia	GMB670T	North Western	H490BND	Walkers	HTJ632P	MTL
GBU3V	MTL	GND502N	Avon Buses	H506BND	A2B Travel	HTJ634P	MTL
GBU10V	MTL	GNF15V	Village	H541EVM	Mercury	HTJ635P	MTL
GDM996X	North Western	GNJ576N	City Bus	H542FWM	Halton	HTJ636P	MTL
GEK12V	Warrington	GNV659N	Nova Scotia	H543FWM	Halton	HTJ637P	MTL
GEK13V	Warrington	GOG99W	North Western	H544FWM	Halton	HTJ639P	MTL
GEK14V	Warrington	GOG116W	North Western	H621BCA	Bostock's	HTJ642P	MTL
GEK15V	Warrington	GOG137W	North Western	H723VWU	Selwyns	HTJ643P	MTL
GEK16V	Warrington	GOG141W	North Western	H794HEM	A2B Travel	HTJ644P	MTL
GFM110X	North Western	GOG144W	North Western	H803RWJ	North Western	HTJ646P	MTL
GHC519N	Warrington	GOG159W	North Western	H804RWJ	North Western	HTJ649P	MTL
GHC522N	Warrington	GOG161W	North Western	H805RWJ	North Western	HTJ654P	MTL
GHC524N	Warrington	GOG248W	North Western	H813JKB	Walkers	HTJ655P	MTL
GHC525N	Warrington	GOG257W	North Western	H829AHS	Roger Hill	HTJ658P	MTL
GHM810N	Bostock's	GOG259W	North Western	H838GLD	MTL	HTJ664P	MTL
GHU643N	North Western	GOG263W	North Western	H839GLD	MTL	HTJ669P	MTL
GIL2403	Ladyline	GOG266W	North Western	H841NOC	Warrington	HTJ670P	MTL
GKA12N	MTL	GSG127T	MTL	H842NOC	Warrington	HTJ674P	MTL
GKA13N	MTL	GSG130T	MTL	H843NOC	Warrington	HTJ682P	MTL
GKA14N	MTL	GTG634W	Town Flyers	H844NOC	Warrington	HTJ685P	MTL
GKA15N	MTL	GTL359N	C M T	H845NOC	Warrington	HVO17V	Arrowbrooke
GKA17N	MTL	GUJ356	Meredith	H846NOC	Warrington	HWJ928W	Happy Al's
GKA20N	MTL	GYE253W	MTL	H847NOC	Warrington	HWJ929W	Happy Al's
GKA21N	MTL	GYE255W	MTL	H879LOX	Warrington	IIL1044	Hardings
GKA22N	MTL	GYE256W	MTL	H881LOX	Warrington	IIL2503	MTL
GKA25N	MTL	GYE257W	MTL	H886LOX	Warrington	J3SLT	South Lancs
GKA26N	MTL	GYE258W	MTL	H887LOX	Warrington	J4SLT	South Lancs
GKA27N	MTL	GYE259W	MTL	H889LOX	Warrington	J5BUS	Jim Stones
GKA35N	MTL	GYE269W	MTL	H897LOX	Warrington	J6SLT	South Lancs
GKA37N	MTL	GYE271W	MTL	H903YUS	Nova Scotia	J7SLT	South Lancs
GKA449L	MTL	GYE276W	MTL	H904YUS	Nova Scotia	J8SLT	South Lancs
GKA454L	MTL	GYE278W	MTL	H905YUS	Nova Scotia	J9SLT	South Lancs
GKA457L	MTL	GYE356W	MTL	HCW762N	MTL	J10SLT	South Lancs
GKA460L	MTL	GYE481W	MTL	HDB124V	Chester	J10WBT	Warrington
GKA461L	MTL	GYE512W	MTL	HED17V	Warrington	J34MKB	MTL
GKA472L	MTL	GYE560W	MTL	HED203V	Halton	J35MKB	MTL
GKA473L	MTL	GYE561W	MTL	HFF234	Ogden's	J44ABC	ABC Travel
GKA477L	MTL	GYE563W	MTL	HFM186N	North Western	J51EDM	Chester
GKA479L	MTL	GYE564W	MTL	HIL2381	Ogden's	J52EDM	Chester
GKA480L	MTL	GYE565W	MTL	HIL3073	Roger Hill	J53EDM	Chester
GKA482L	MTL	GYE570W	MTL	HIL3478	Roger Hill	J54EDM	Chester
GKA486M	MTL	GYE571W	MTL	HIL3931	Huxley	J55ABC	ABC Travel
GKA488M	MTL	GYE572W	MTL	HIL3932	Huxley	J55BUS	Jim Stones
GKA489M	MTL	GYE574W	MTL	HIL3934	Huxley	J78MHF	North Western
GKA490M	MTL	GYE576W	MTL	HIL3935	Huxley	J136OBU	Ogden's
GKA491M	MTL	GYE578W	MTL	HIL5697	MTL	J155EDM	Chester
GKA492M	MTL	GYE579W	MTL	HIL5698	MTL	J210BWU	MTL
GKA493M	MTL	GYE588W	MTL	HIL6956	Ogden's	J211BWU	MTL
GKA498M	MTL	GYE594W	MTL	HIL6975	MTL	J212BWU	MTL
GKA501M	MTL	H1JYM	Jim Stones	HJI843	Meredith	J213BWU	MTL
GKA507M	MTL	H4ABC	ABC Travel	HKF151	Aintree Coachlines	J214BWU	MTL
GKA508M	MTL	H6CLW	Happy Al's	HMA104X	Chester	J215BWU	MTL
GKA511M	MTL	H7CLW	Happy Al's	HMA105X	Chester	J216BWU	MTL
GKA513M	MTL	H11JYM	Halton Mini	HMA106X	Chester	J217BWU	MTL
GKA515M	MTL	H14JYM	Halton Mini	HMA559T	North Western	J218BWU	MTL
GKA516M	MTL	H34HBG	Halton	HMA567T	North Western	J219BWU	MTL
GKA517M	MTL	H35HBG	Halton	HMA568T	North Western	J220BWU	MTL
GKA518M	MTL	H81PTG	North Western	HOI2804	Huxley	J221BWU	MTL
GKA524M	MTL	H85PTG	North Western	HOI7544	Walkers	J249KWM	Halton

J250KWM	Halton	JJD479D	MTL	K130TCP	MTL	KFF257	MTL
J251KWM	Halton	JJD511D	MTL	K131TCP	MTL	KFM190T	Chester
J256MFP	Bostock's	JJD561D	MTL	K132TCP	MTL	KFM192T	Chester
J291NNB	North Western	JJG908P	City Bus	K133TCP	MTL	KFM193T	Chester
J292NNB	North Western	JJP335V	Bennett's	K200SLT	North Western	KGH969A	A1A Travel
J293NNB	North Western	JKB146L	Village	K221VTB	Warrington	KGJ167A	MTL
J296NNB	North Western	JMB406T	North Western	K222VTB	Warrington	KHH374W	MTL
J297NNB	North Western	JNH184Y	Nip-On	K223VTB	Warrington	KHJ999	Grand Edwardian
J298NNB	North Western	JOI2949	Ogden's	K224VTB	Warrington	KJD80P	Village
J299NNB	North Western	JOX515P	North Western	K225VTB	Warrington	KJO503W	Happy Al's
J332LVM	Dobson's	JOX520P	North Western	K333DOT	Ogden's	KJO506W	Happy Al's
J387PVR	Dobson's	JOX522P	North Western	K400ABC	ABC Travel	KJO508W	Happy Al's
J410AWF	Warrington	JSL282X	Chester	K423THG	Wingates	KJO509W	Happy Al's
J414AWF	Warrington	JSL283X	Chester	K427THG	Wingates	KJW281W	North Western
J444ABC	ABC Travel	JSL284X	Chester	K456PNR	Bostock's	KJW284W	North Western
J531JNH	MTL	JSV343	City Bus	K457EVC	North Western	KJW287W	North Western
J628LHF	Halton	JTU226T	Bostock's	K476FYN	MTL	KJW288W	North Western
J629LHF	Halton	JTU228T	Bostock's	K504WNR	Express Travel	KLG106Y	Bostock's
J630LHF	Halton	JTU230T	Bostock's	K505WNR	Express Travel	KLG107Y	Chester
J644LKD	North Western	JTU582T	North Western	K506WNR	Express Travel	KLG108Y	Chester
J692LGA	Bostock's	JTU583T	North Western	K510FYN	MTL	KLG109Y	Chester
J708MSD	Whitegate	JUH227W	Nip-On	K510RJX	MTL	KMA395T	North Western
J734MFY	North Western	JUM501V	MTL	K555ANT	Anthony's Travel	KMA396T	North Western
J735MFY	North Western	JUM502V	MTL	K762FYG	Selwyns	KMA397T	North Western
J800ABC	ABC Travel	JUM503V	MTL	K782VNF	City Bus	KMA400T	North Western
J810HMC	MTL	JUM504V	MTL	K787VNR	North Western	KMA403T	North Western
J811HMC	MTL	JUM505V	MTL	K801NTJ	MTL	KMA412T	North Western
J812HMC	MTL	JWM687P	MTL	K802NTJ	MTL	KNH500N	C M T
J813HMC	MTL	JWM689P	MTL	K803NTJ	MTL	KNK369H	A2B Travel
J814HMC	MTL	JWM693P	MTL	K804NTJ	MTL	KNV514P	North Western
J815HMC	MTL	JWM694P	MTL	K805NTJ	MTL	KON372P	Village
J816HMC	MTL	JWM695P	MTL	K806NTJ	MTL	KRP564V	C M T
J817HMC	MTL	JWM696P	MTL	K817NKH	MTL	KSD91W	Happy Al's
J818HMC	MTL	JWM698P	MTL	K818NKH	MTL	KSD97W	Happy Al's
J819HMC	MTL	JWM700P	MTL	K819NKH	MTL	KSD102W	Happy Al's
J820HMC	MTL	JWM701P	MTL	K820NKH	MTL	KSV408	Meredith
J821HMC	MTL	JWM702P	MTL	K821NKH	MTL	KWJ136P	Village
J910OEY	Selwyns	JWM703P	MTL	K822NKH	MTL	KYN284X	MTL
J921MKC	Halton	JWM704P	MTL	K823NKH	MTL	KYN289X	MTL
J922MKC	Halton	JWM705P	MTL	K824NKH	MTL	KYN290X	MTL
J923MKC	Halton	JWM706P	MTL	K825NKH	MTL	KYN293X	MTL
J924MKC	Halton	JWM710P	MTL	K826NKH	MTL	KYN299X	MTL
J925MKC	Halton	JWM713P	MTL	K827NKH	MTL	KYN301X	MTL
J926MKC	Halton	JWM714P	MTL	K828NKH	MTL	KYN303X	MTL
J927MKC	Halton	JWM715P	MTL	K829OKH	MTL	KYN304X	MTL
J928MKC	Halton	JWM717P	MTL	K830OKH	MTL	KYN315X	MTL
J929MKC	Halton	JWM720P	MTL	K831OKH	MTL	KYN316X	MTL
J988TVU	South Lancs	JWM721P	MTL	K832OKH	MTL	KYO608X	MTL
JBO74W	MTL	JWM722P	MTL	K833OKH	MTL	KYO616X	MTL
JBO76W	MTL	JWM723P	MTL	K834OKH	MTL	KYO620X	MTL
JBO77W	MTL	JWM724P	MTL	K835OKH	MTL	KYO623X	MTL
JBO78W	MTL	K1SLT	South Lancs	K836OKH	MTL	KYV324X	MTL
JBO79W	MTL	K2SLT	South Lancs	K837OKH	MTL	KYV330X	MTL
JBO81W	MTL	K3SEL	Selwyns	K852MTJ	Halton	KYV332X	MTL
JBO350N	C M T	K3SLT	South Lancs	K853MTJ	Halton	KYV333X	MTL
JBO351N	C M T	K18AMB	Express Travel	K876UDB	North Western	KYV337X	MTL
JBR687T	Nova Scotia	K19AMB	Express Travel	K877UDB	North Western	KYV338X	MTL
JCK851W	North Western	K20AMB	Express Travel	K878UDB	North Western	KYV339X	MTL
JCM396	Meredith	K22ANT	Anthony's Travel	K879UDB	North Western	KYV344X	MTL
JED904	Meredith	K56LLG	Chester	K880UDB	North Western	KYV347X	MTL
JFM220D	North Western	K57LLG	Chester	K882UDB	North Western	KYV350X	MTL
JGH118X	MTL	K58LLG	Chester	K884UDB	North Western	KYV351X	MTL
JHE144W	MTL	K59LLG	Chester	K887UDB	North Western	KYV353X	MTL
JHE152W	MTL	K100SLT	North Western	K890UDB	North Western	KYV354X	MTL
JHE156W	MTL	K101OHF	MTL	K911OEM	MTL	KYV355X	MTL
JHF824	Walkers	K102OHF	MTL	K945OEM	MTL	KYV359X	MTL
JHF825	Walkers	K103OHF	MTL	K946OEM	MTL	KYV363X	MTL
JHF826	Walkers	K104OHF	MTL	K947OEM	MTL	KYV364X	MTL
JJD367D	MTL	K105OHF	MTL	K948OEM	MTL	KYV365X	MTL
JJD393D	MTL	K106OHF	MTL	K949OEM	MTL	KYV367X	MTL
JJD395D	MTL	K106RNS	Lofty's	K955PBG	MTL	KYV374X	MTL
JJD413D	MTL	K107OHF	MTL	KBV146S	Roger Hill	KYV376X	MTL
JJD419D	MTL	K108OHF	MTL	KEH976N	Roger Hill	KYV382X	MTL

Reg	Operator	Reg	Operator	Reg	Operator	Reg	Operator
KYV383X	MTL	L61PDM	Chester	L218TKA	MTL	L512TKA	MTL
KYV385X	MTL	L62PDM	Chester	L219TKA	MTL	L513TKA	MTL
KYV389X	MTL	L63SFM	Chester	L220TKA	MTL	L529XVR	North Western
KYV391X	MTL	L64SFM	Chester	L221TKA	MTL	L532EHD	North Western
KYV393X	MTL	L99ABC	ABC Travel	L222TKA	MTL	L532EHD	North Western
KYV398X	MTL	L101HHV	MTL	L223TKA	MTL	L641DNA	North Western
KYV400X	MTL	L102HHV	MTL	L224TKA	MTL	L642DNA	North Western
KYV402X	MTL	L103HHV	MTL	L225TKA	MTL	L643DNA	North Western
KYV407X	MTL	L104HHV	MTL	L226SWM	Warrington	L644DNA	North Western
KYV409X	MTL	L105HHV	MTL	L226TKA	MTL	L646DNA	North Western
KYV412X	MTL	L106HHV	MTL	L227SWM	Warrington	L648DNA	North Western
KYV413X	MTL	L107HHV	MTL	L227TKA	MTL	L649DNA	North Western
KYV414X	MTL	L108HHV	MTL	L228SWM	Warrington	L700ABC	ABC Travel
KYV416X	MTL	L109HHV	MTL	L228TKA	MTL	L705PHE	Express Travel
KYV417X	MTL	L110HHV	MTL	L229SWM	Warrington	L706PHE	Express Travel
KYV418X	MTL	L111ANT	Anthony's Travel	L229TKA	MTL	L707PHE	Express Travel
KYV421X	MTL	L112HHV	MTL	L230SWM	Warrington	L708PHE	Express Travel
KYV424X	MTL	L113HHV	MTL	L230TKA	MTL	L709PHE	Express Travel
KYV425X	MTL	L114HHV	MTL	L231SWM	Warrington	L710PHE	Express Travel
KYV426X	MTL	L115HHV	MTL	L231TKA	MTL	L711PHE	Express Travel
KYV427X	MTL	L116HHV	MTL	L232SWM	Warrington	L712PHE	Express Travel
KYV430X	MTL	L117HHV	MTL	L232TKA	MTL	L713PHE	Express Travel
KYV431X	MTL	L118HHV	MTL	L233SWM	Warrington	L714PHE	Express Travel
KYV436X	MTL	L119HHV	MTL	L233TKA	MTL	L805YBC	A2B Travel
KYV440X	MTL	L120HHV	MTL	L234SWM	Warrington	L806YBC	A2B Travel
KYV443X	MTL	L150SBG	North Western	L234TKA	MTL	L807TFY	MTL
KYV449X	MTL	L151SBG	North Western	L235SWM	Warrington	L808TFY	MTL
KYV450X	MTL	L152SBG	North Western	L235TKA	MTL	L809TFY	MTL
KYV463X	MTL	L153UEM	North Western	L236TKA	MTL	L810TFY	MTL
KYV464X	MTL	L153UKB	North Western	L237TKA	MTL	L899LFS	A1A Travel
KYV468X	MTL	L154UEM	North Western	L238TKA	MTL	L970VGE	Lofty's
KYV472X	MTL	L154UKB	North Western	L239TKA	MTL	L973KDT	Hardings
KYV483X	MTL	L155UEM	North Western	L240TKA	MTL	L999ABC	ABC Travel
KYV484X	MTL	L155UKB	North Western	L241TKA	MTL	LBP196P	North Western
KYV489X	MTL	L156UEM	North Western	L242TKA	MTL	LCA182X	Bostock's
KYV491X	MTL	L156UKB	North Western	L243TKA	MTL	LCA183X	Bostock's
KYV494X	MTL	L160PDM	Chester	L244TKA	MTL	LCW731W	City Bus
KYV499X	MTL	L177PDO	A2B Travel	L245TKA	MTL	LDM441Y	Arrowbrooke
KYV509X	MTL	L193DBC	North Western	L246TKA	MTL	LEC751X	Acorn Travel
KYV520X	MTL	L201SKD	MTL	L247TKA	MTL	LED70P	Warrington
KYV528X	MTL	L201TKA	MTL	L248TKA	MTL	LED71P	Warrington
KYV534X	MTL	L202SKD	MTL	L249TKA	MTL	LED72P	Warrington
KYV538X	MTL	L202TKA	MTL	L250TKA	MTL	LED73P	Warrington
KYV547X	MTL	L203SKD	MTL	L301TEM	MTL	LFR125T	Warrington
KYV639X	MTL	L203TKA	MTL	L302TEM	MTL	LFR126T	Warrington
KYV640X	MTL	L204SKD	MTL	L303TEM	MTL	LFR854X	North Western
KYV656X	MTL	L204TKA	MTL	L401LHE	Hardings	LFR863X	MTL
KYV674X	MTL	L205SKD	MTL	L402LHE	Hardings	LFR867X	North Western
KYV677X	MTL	L205TKA	MTL	L402TKB	MTL	LFR869X	North Western
KYV678X	MTL	L206SKD	MTL	L403LHE	Hardings	LFR872X	MTL
KYV693X	MTL	L206TKA	MTL	L403TKB	MTL	LGV444	Grand Edwardian
KYV739X	MTL	L207SKD	MTL	L404TKB	MTL	LIL2258	Huxley
KYV755X	MTL	L207TKA	MTL	L405TKB	MTL	LIL4019	Huxley
KYV764X	MTL	L208SKD	MTL	L406TKB	MTL	LIL4398	Huxley
KYV797X	MTL	L208TKA	MTL	L407TKB	MTL	LIW6076	Anthony's Travel
KYV800X	MTL	L209SKD	MTL	L408TKB	MTL	LKF726R	MTL
KYV801X	MTL	L209TKA	MTL	L409TKB	MTL	LKF727R	MTL
KYV803X	MTL	L210SKD	MTL	L410TKB	MTL	LKF728R	MTL
KYV804X	MTL	L210TKA	MTL	L411UFY	MTL	LKF730R	MTL
L1BUS	A1A Travel	L211SBG	MTL	L412UFY	MTL	LKF731R	MTL
L1SLT	South Lancs	L211TKA	MTL	L413TKB	MTL	LKF734R	MTL
L2BUS	A1A Travel	L212TKA	MTL	L483DOA	Dobson's	LKF735R	MTL
L2SLT	South Lancs	L212TWM	MTL	L501TKA	MTL	LKF736R	MTL
L3SLT	North Western	L213TKA	MTL	L502TKA	MTL	LKF737R	MTL
L5ABC	ABC Travel	L213TWM	MTL	L503TKA	MTL	LKF738R	MTL
L5BUS	Jim Stones	L214TKA	MTL	L504TKA	MTL	LKF740R	MTL
L5HMC	Village	L214TWM	MTL	L505TKA	MTL	LKF741R	MTL
L6ABC	ABC Travel	L215TKA	MTL	L506TKA	MTL	LKF742R	MTL
L10GGY	Ogden's	L215TWM	MTL	L507TKA	MTL	LKF743R	MTL
L11SLT	South Lancs	L216TKA	MTL	L508TKA	MTL	LKF744R	MTL
L22AJB	City Bus	L216TWM	MTL	L509TKA	MTL	LKF745R	MTL
L35AKP	A2B Travel	L217TKA	MTL	L510TKA	MTL	LKF747R	MTL
L55BUS	Jim Stones	L217TWM	MTL	L511TKA	MTL	LKF748R	MTL

LKF749R	MTL	M127YCM	North Western	M219AKB	North Western	M533WHF	MTL
LKF750R	MTL	M128YCM	North Western	M219YKC	MTL	M534WHF	MTL
LKF751R	MTL	M129YCM	North Western	M220AKB	North Western	M535WHF	MTL
LKF752R	MTL	M157WKA	North Western	M221AKB	North Western	M536WHF	MTL
LKF753R	MTL	M157WWM	North Western	M223AKB	North Western	M537WHF	MTL
LKF754R	MTL	M158WKA	North Western	M224AKB	North Western	M538WHF	MTL
LKF755R	MTL	M158WWM	North Western	M225AKB	North Western	M539WHF	MTL
LOA332X	North Western	M159WKA	North Western	M226AKB	North Western	M540WHF	MTL
LOA416X	North Western	M160WKA	North Western	M227AKB	North Western	M541WHF	MTL
LOA419X	North Western	M160WTJ	North Western	M228AKB	North Western	M542WHF	MTL
LOA420X	North Western	M161WKA	North Western	M229AKB	North Western	M543WHF	MTL
LOA426X	North Western	M162WKA	North Western	M230AKB	North Western	M544WTJ	MTL
LOA428X	North Western	M163WKA	North Western	M231AKB	North Western	M545WTJ	MTL
LOA430X	North Western	M164WKA	North Western	M232AKB	North Western	M546WTJ	MTL
LOA432X	North Western	M165WKA	North Western	M236YKD	Warrington	M547WTJ	MTL
LOA434X	North Western	M165XMA	Chester	M237YKD	Warrington	M548WTJ	MTL
LOA435X	North Western	M166WKA	North Western	M238YKD	Warrington	M549WTJ	MTL
LPB195P	North Western	M166WTJ	North Western	M239XLV	North Western	M550WTJ	MTL
LPB205P	North Western	M166XMA	Chester	M239YCM	Warrington	M551WTJ	MTL
LPB207P	North Western	M167WKA	North Western	M240XLV	North Western	M552WTJ	MTL
LPB209P	North Western	M168WKA	North Western	M240YCM	Warrington	M553WTJ	MTL
LPB212P	C M T	M169WKA	North Western	M241YCM	Warrington	M554WTJ	MTL
LPB219P	North Western	M170WKA	North Western	M242YCM	Warrington	M556WTJ	MTL
LPB221P	C M T	M171YKA	North Western	M243YCM	Warrington	M557WTJ	MTL
LPB222P	C M T	M172YKA	North Western	M246YWM	Warrington	M558WTJ	MTL
LPB225P	North Western	M173YKA	North Western	M247YLV	Warrington	M559WTJ	MTL
LPY458W	South Lancs	M174YKA	North Western	M248YLV	Warrington	M561WTJ	MTL
LPY462W	South Lancs	M175YKA	North Western	M252SRN	Ogden's	M562WTJ	MTL
LRB202W	North Western	M176YKA	North Western	M255BDM	Selwyns	M563WTJ	MTL
LUA311V	MTL	M177YKA	North Western	M284HRH	Warrington	M564YEM	MTL
LUA325V	City Bus	M178YKA	North Western	M301YBG	MTL	M565YEM	MTL
LUA330V	Nip-On	M179YKA	North Western	M302YBG	MTL	M566YEM	MTL
M1BUS	Jim Stones	M180YKA	North Western	M303YBG	MTL	M567YEM	MTL
M2SLT	North Western	M181YKA	North Western	M322AKB	North Western	M568YEM	MTL
M3ERH	Roger Hill	M182YKA	North Western	M363KVR	North Western	M569YEM	MTL
M4JBA	A1A Travel	M183YKA	North Western	M364KVR	North Western	M570YEM	MTL
M6SEL	Selwyns	M184YKA	North Western	M365AMA	Selwyns	M571YEM	MTL
M7ABC	ABC Travel	M185YKA	North Western	M365KVR	North Western	M572YEM	MTL
M7SEL	Selwyns	M186YKA	North Western	M366AMA	Selwyns	M573YEM	MTL
M13BUS	A1A Travel	M187YKA	North Western	M366KVR	North Western	M574YEM	MTL
M15BUS	Jim Stones	M188YKA	North Western	M367AMA	Selwyns	M575YEM	MTL
M20GGY	MTL	M189YKA	North Western	M367KVR	North Western	M579WLV	Halton
M30GGY	MTL	M190YKA	North Western	M368KVR	North Western	M580WLV	Halton
M55BUS	Jim Stones	M191YKA	North Western	M369KVR	North Western	M581WLV	Halton
M59WKA	North Western	M192YKA	North Western	M370KVR	North Western	M582WLV	Halton
M61WKA	North Western	M193YKA	North Western	M371KVR	North Western	M583WLV	Halton
M62WKA	North Western	M194YKA	North Western	M372KVR	North Western	M584WLV	Halton
M63WKA	North Western	M195YKA	North Western	M385KVR	North Western	M593HKH	Warrington
M64WKA	North Western	M196YKA	North Western	M390KVR	Selwyns	M602BCA	Selwyns
M65WKA	North Western	M197YKA	North Western	M392KVR	North Western	M615XLG	North Western
M67WKA	North Western	M198YKA	North Western	M393KVR	North Western	M647YLV	C M T
M71AKA	Halton	M199YKA	North Western	M394KVR	North Western	M648YLV	C M T
M73AKA	Halton	M201YKA	North Western	M423TJO	Whitegate	M649YLV	C M T
M74AKA	Halton	M202YKA	North Western	M441BDM	Selwyns	M650YLV	C M T
M77ABC	ABC Travel	M203YKA	North Western	M514WHF	MTL	M689FJF	North Western
M87DEW	Halton	M204YKA	North Western	M515WHF	MTL	M777ABC	ABC Travel
M89DEW	Halton	M205YKA	North Western	M516WHF	MTL	M799HPJ	Selwyns
M101WKA	North Western	M206YKA	North Western	M517WHF	MTL	M841RCP	North Western
M102WKA	North Western	M207PAN	Hardings	M518WHF	MTL	M842RCP	North Western
M103WKA	North Western	M207YKA	North Western	M519WHF	MTL	M843RCP	North Western
M104WKA	North Western	M208PAN	Hardings	M520WHF	MTL	M878DDS	Lofty's
M105WKA	North Western	M208YKA	North Western	M521WHF	MTL	M880DDS	Lofty's
M109XKC	MTL	M209YKA	North Western	M522WHF	MTL	M998XRF	North Western
M110XKC	MTL	M210YKA	North Western	M523WHF	MTL	MAR781P	North Western
M112XKC	MTL	M211YKD	North Western	M524WHF	MTL	MCA675T	North Western
M113XKC	MTL	M212YKD	North Western	M525WHF	MTL	MCA678T	North Western
M120YCM	North Western	M213YKD	North Western	M526WHF	MTL	MCN30K	MTL
M121YCM	North Western	M214YKD	North Western	M527WHF	MTL	MCU98K	Acorn Travel
M122YCM	North Western	M215YKD	North Western	M528WHF	MTL	MDL880R	Halton
M123YCM	North Western	M216YKD	North Western	M529WHF	MTL	MEF825W	City Bus
M124YCM	North Western	M217AKB	North Western	M530WHF	MTL	MEK18W	Warrington
M125YCM	North Western	M218AKB	North Western	M531WHF	MTL	MEK19W	Warrington
M126YCM	North Western	M218YKC	MTL	M532WHF	MTL	MEK20W	Warrington

BFV900R appears in the book under the Nip-On fleet where it arrived during 1995. Pictured here in the colours of South Lancs it shows the style of the Duple Dominant bus body in this example built on a Leyland Leopard chassis and which was new to Rhymney Valley. *Paul Wigan*

MEK21W	Warrington	N238CKA	North Western	N283CKB	MTL	N585CKA	MTL
MEK22W	Warrington	N239CKA	North Western	N284CKB	MTL	N586CKA	MTL
MEK23W	Warrington	N240CKA	North Western	N285CKB	MTL	N587CKA	MTL
MFE504	Huxley	N241CKA	North Western	N286CKB	MTL	N588CKA	MTL
MLJ919P	North Western	N242CKA	North Western	N287CKB	MTL	N589CKA	MTL
MNH571V	C M T	N243CKA	North Western	N288CKB	MTL	N590CKA	MTL
MNH576V	C M T	N244CKA	North Western	N289CKB	MTL	N591CKA	MTL
MNS44Y	Happy Al's	N245CKA	North Western	N291CKB	MTL	N592CKA	MTL
MNS46Y	Happy Al's	N246CKA	North Western	N292CKB	MTL	N593CKA	MTL
MNS48Y	Happy Al's	N247CKA	North Western	N293CKB	MTL	N594CKA	MTL
MNS51Y	Happy Al's	N248CKA	North Western	N294CKB	MTL	N595CKA	MTL
MNY892X	Nip-On	N249CKA	North Western	N295CKB	MTL	N596CKA	MTL
MPN140W	Chester	N250CKA	North Western	N296CKB	MTL	N597CKA	MTL
MPN141W	Chester	N251CKA	North Western	N297CKB	MTL	N598CKA	MTL
MTJ758S	MTL	N252CKA	North Western	N298CKB	MTL	N599CKA	MTL
MTJ759S	MTL	N253CKA	North Western	N299CKB	MTL	N600ABC	ABC Travel
MTJ760S	MTL	N254CKA	North Western	N301CKB	MTL	N601CKA	MTL
MTJ761S	MTL	N255CKA	North Western	N302CKB	MTL	N602CKA	MTL
MTJ762S	MTL	N256CKA	North Western	N303CKB	MTL	N603CKA	MTL
MTJ764S	MTL	N257CKA	North Western	N304CKB	MTL	N604CKA	MTL
MVM33W	Ladyline	N258CKA	North Western	N305CKB	MTL	N605CKA	MTL
MWW561P	Wingates	N259CKA	North Western	N306CKB	MTL	N606CKA	MTL
N8ABC	ABC Travel	N260CKA	North Western	N307CLV	MTL	N607CKA	MTL
N9ABC	ABC Travel	N261CKA	North Western	N308CLV	MTL	N608CKA	MTL
N41BWM	MTL	N262CKA	North Western	N31FWU	Happy Al's	N609CKA	MTL
N42BWM	MTL	N263CKA	North Western	N32FWU	Happy Al's	N610CKA	MTL
N101YVU	North Western	N264CKA	North Western	N491MGG	Lofty's	N611CKA	MTL
N102YVU	North Western	N271CKB	MTL	N492MGG	Lofty's	N612CKA	MTL
N103YVU	North Western	N272CKB	MTL	N493MGG	Lofty's	N613CKA	MTL
N104YVU	North Western	N273CKB	MTL	N576CKA	MTL	N014CKA	MTL
N105YVU	North Western	N274CKB	MTL	N577CKA	MTL	N615CKA	MTL
N205VRX	Hardings	N275CKB	MTL	N578CKA	MTL	N616CKA	MTL
N206VRX	Hardings	N276CKB	MTL	N579CKA	MTL	N617CKA	MTL
N233CKA	North Western	N277CKB	MTL	N580CKA	MTL	N618CKA	MTL
N234CKA	North Western	N278CKB	MTL	N581CKA	MTL	N619CKA	MTL
N235CKA	North Western	N279CKB	MTL	N582CKA	MTL	N620CKA	MTL
N236CKA	North Western	N281CKB	MTL	N583CKA	MTL	N621CKA	MTL
N237CKA	North Western	N282CKB	MTL	N584CKA	MTL	N622CKA	MTL

Liverline's new livery scheme is white with two shades of blue in similar proportions to the North Western main scheme. Seen heading south through Liverpool is 730, VPA150S a Leyland Atlantean with Park Royal bodywork acquired by North Western from London & Country in 1991.

N623CKA	MTL	NHH379W	MTL	NUW612Y	MTL	OJD879Y	MTL
N624CKA	MTL	NHH381W	MTL	NUW628Y	MTL	OJD890Y	MTL
N625CKA	MTL	NJI9479	MTL	NUW638Y	MTL	OJD896Y	MTL
N626CKA	MTL	NKY142R	Village	NUW655Y	MTL	OJV122S	Bennett's
N652CHF	C M T	NML603E	MTL	NUW656Y	MTL	OKY62R	Village
N653CHF	C M T	NML620E	MTL	OCO107S	North Western	OLG7	Meredith
N654CHF	C M T	NMY655E	MTL	OCO109S	North Western	OLV551M	MTL
N655CHF	C M T	NNO65P	North Western	OCS34X	Chester	OMA510V	North Western
N656CHF	C M T	NOC444R	Merseyline	ODL883R	Halton	OMB619P	Bostock's
N657CHF	C M T	NOC445R	Merseyline	ODL884R	Halton	ONF658R	MTL
N658CHF	C M T	NOC489R	Village	ODL886R	Halton	ONF670R	MTL
N671CLV	Halton	NOC585R	Merseyline	ODM193P	Bostock's	ONF671R	MTL
N672CLV	Halton	NOC598R	Village	ODM680V	North Western	ONF675R	MTL
N673CLV	Halton	NOC726R	Village	OED3W	A1A Travel	ONF678R	MTL
N811CKA	MTL	NOC734R	Village	OFM957K	Chester	ONF693R	MTL
N935ETU	Lofty's	NOE557R	Nova Scotia	OFR930T	Arrowbrooke	ONF694R	MTL
N936ETU	Lofty's	NOE592R	North Western	OHF858S	Aintree Coachlines	OPV893W	Ladyline
N998KUS	Lofty's	NPA227W	Nip-On	OHV682Y	MTL	OTB24W	Warrington
NAX511	Meredith	NPA232W	Nip-On	OHV690Y	MTL	OTB25W	Warrington
NDZ7918	MTL	NPK232R	C M T	OHV692Y	MTL	OTB26W	Warrington
NDZ7919	MTL	NPK233R	North Western	OHV695Y	MTL	OTB27W	Warrington
NDZ7920	MTL	NPK242R	North Western	OHV698Y	MTL	OTB28W	Warrington
NDZ7921	MTL	NPK245R	North Western	OHV703Y	MTL	OTX59R	Arrowbrooke
NDZ7922	MTL	NPK249R	C M T	OHV726Y	MTL	OYM453A	MTL
NDZ7923	MTL	NPK250R	North Western	OHV730Y	MTL	PBL495T	North Western
NDZ7924	MTL	NPK258R	North Western	OHV733Y	MTL	PCA422V	North Western
NDZ7925	MTL	NPK259R	North Western	OHV741Y	MTL	PCA423V	North Western
NDZ7926	MTL	NPK263R	North Western	OHV746Y	MTL	PCA424V	North Western
NDZ7927	MTL	NSU572	Hardings	OHV753Y	MTL	PCA425V	North Western
NDZ7928	MTL	NSU573	Hardings	OHV754Y	MTL	PEV695R	C M T
NDZ7929	MTL	NTC443M	Bennett's	OIA773	A1A Travel	PFC511W	Happy Al's
NDZ7930	MTL	NTU11Y	North Western	OIJ2645	Ogden's	PFC513W	Happy Al's
NDZ7931	MTL	NTU12Y	North Western	OIW5804	MTL	PFM126Y	North Western
NDZ7932	MTL	NTU13Y	North Western	OJD168R	MTL	PFM128Y	North Western
NDZ7933	MTL	NTU15Y	North Western	OJD824Y	MTL	PFM129Y	North Western
NDZ7934	MTL	NUW561Y	MTL	OJD829Y	MTL	PHN570R	South Lancs
NDZ7935	MTL	NUW570Y	MTL	OJD876Y	MTL	PHN571R	South Lancs
NGR683P	South Lancs	NUW599Y	MTL	OJD878Y	MTL	PHN572R	South Lancs

Reg	Operator	Reg	Operator	Reg	Operator	Reg	Operator
PIB5898	Anthony's Travel	RUK522L	Walkers	SFV433P	North Western	TOE489N	North Western
PJI5913	MTL	RVN243X	Nip-On	SFV436P	North Western	TOE490N	North Western
PJI5916	MTL	RWT548R	Dobson's	SMB601V	Bostock's	TOE491N	North Western
PJT272R	C M T	SCD731N	North Western	SMB602V	Bostock's	TOE497N	North Western
PKB555M	MTL	SCH153X	Wingates	SMK679F	MTL	TOE498N	North Western
PKP551R	North Western	SCK688P	North Western	SMK699F	MTL	TOH2S	Wingates
PRJ493R	MTL	SCK689P	North Western	SMK731F	MTL	TPU70R	North Western
PRR106L	Walkers	SCK692P	North Western	SPC266R	C M T	TPU72R	North Western
PRR108L	Walkers	SCK693P	North Western	SPC267R	C M T	TRN466V	North Western
PRR110L	Walkers	SCK694P	C M T	SPC278R	C M T	TSU610	Selwyns
PTD672S	Nip-On	SCK696P	C M T	SPC279R	North Western	TTB74S	Warrington
PTX466Y	Arrowbrooke	SCK698P	North Western	SPC284R	C M T	TTB76S	Warrington
PUA506W	MTL	SCK699P	North Western	SPC286R	C M T	TTB78S	Warrington
PUA508W	MTL	SCK700P	North Western	SPC291R	C M T	TTB79S	Warrington
PUA510W	MTL	SCK706P	North Western	SRJ731R	MTL	TTB80S	Warrington
PUK638R	North Western	SCK710P	North Western	SRJ732R	MTL	TTB81S	Warrington
PUK640R	North Western	SCS363M	Meredith	SRJ742R	MTL	TTB82S	Warrington
PUP505T	North Western	SCS365M	Meredith	SRJ749R	MTL	TTB83S	Warrington
PUP565T	A1A Travel	SCW103X	Chester	SRJ752R	MTL	TUB250R	Aintree Coachlines
PYM106F	Grand Edwardian	SCW104X	Chester	SRJ753R	MTL	TWH694T	Chester
PYM108F	Grand Edwardian	SDA557S	Merseyline	SRJ754R	MTL	TWH703T	Merseyline
RAW35R	Bennett's	SDA564S	Merseyline	STU260L	Bostock's	TWH704T	Merseyline
RBG821T	MTL	SDA565S	Merseyline	SVL174W	City Bus	TWJ340Y	Warrington
RBG825T	MTL	SDA638S	Merseyline	SXI9035	A1A Travel	TWJ341Y	Warrington
RBG826T	MTL	SDA641S	Village	TCK821	ABC Travel	TWJ342Y	Warrington
RBG827T	MTL	SDA644S	Village	TEC599N	Jim Stones	TWM209V	MTL
RBG837T	MTL	SDA658S	Village	TEH442W	Roger Hill	TWM210V	MTL
RBG839T	MTL	SDA709S	Merseyline	THX253S	C M T	TWM211V	MTL
RBG840T	MTL	SDA712S	Merseyline	THX556S	MTL	TWM212V	MTL
RBG841T	MTL	SDA767S	Merseyline	TIB2387	Anthony's Travel	TWM213V	MTL
RCH283R	Village	SDA768S	Merseyline	TJI1690	Taylors	TWM214V	MTL
RCH285R	Village	SDA772S	Merseyline	TJI1691	Taylors	TWM216V	MTL
RCH286R	Village	SDA778S	Merseyline	TJI1692	Taylors	TWM217V	MTL
RCH288R	Village	SDA784S	Merseyline	TJI1693	Taylors	TWM219V	MTL
REK75R	Warrington	SDC146H	Avon Buses	TJI1694	Taylors	TWM220V	MTL
REK77R	Warrington	SDM94V	Chester	TJI1695	Taylors	TWM221V	MTL
RFR409P	North Western	SDM95V	Chester	TJI1696	Ladyline	TWS907T	Happy Al's
RFR414P	North Western	SDM96V	Chester	TJI3369	Taylors	UBV92L	Village
RFR423P	North Western	SDM97V	Chester	TJI3372	Taylors	UEM35V	MTL
RIB4310	Village	SDM98V	Chester	TJI3373	Taylors	UEM36V	MTL
RJA723R	MTL	SEL23	Selwyns	TJI3374	Taylors	UEM37V	MTL
RKA589N	MTL	SEL36	Selwyns	TJI6325	Taylors	UEM38V	MTL
RLG427V	North Western	SEL73	Selwyns	TJI6326	Taylors	UEM39V	MTL
RLS468T	Meredith	SEL133	Selwyns	TMX535R	Aintree Coachlines	UEM40V	MTL
RMA437V	North Western	SEL392	Selwyns	TOE468N	North Western	UEM41V	MTL
RMA439V	North Western	SEL853	Selwyns	TOE469N	North Western	UFG61S	C M T
RSG817V	MTL	SFV427P	North Western	TOE486N	North Western	UFV113R	Warrington
RUA453W	Happy Al's	SFV428P	North Western	TOE487N	North Western	UFV116R	Warrington
RUF45R	C M T	SFV432P	North Western	TOE488N	North Western	UFV117R	Warrington

Selwyns have used SELxxx marks for many years. Here seen on a Dennis Javelin with Plaxton Premiére bodywork for National Express duties is M7SEL purchased from DVLA.

Reg	Operator	Reg	Operator	Reg	Operator	Reg	Operator
UFV120R	Warrington	VCA456W	North Western	WWM911W	MTL	XEM909W	MTL
UGB24V	Happy Al's	VCA463W	North Western	WWM912W	MTL	XEM910W	MTL
UHG718R	C M T	VCU368T	MTL	WWM913W	MTL	XEM911W	MTL
UHG724R	North Western	VCU369T	MTL	WWM914W	MTL	XEM912W	MTL
UHG735R	North Western	VCU374T	MTL	WWM915W	MTL	XFM211	Chester
UHG751R	North Western	VCU375T	MTL	WWM916W	MTL	XLV139W	MTL
UHG759R	North Western	VCU376T	MTL	WWM924W	MTL	XLV140W	MTL
UHG760R	North Western	VCU377T	MTL	WWO640T	Dobson's	XLV141W	MTL
UIA826	A2B Travel	VCU378T	MTL	WYJ170S	C M T	XLV142W	MTL
UKA19V	MTL	VCU379T	MTL	WYV44T	MTL	XLV143W	MTL
UKA20V	MTL	VCU381T	MTL	WYV45T	MTL	XLV144W	MTL
UKA21V	MTL	VCU384T	MTL	WYV46T	MTL	XLV145W	MTL
UKA22V	MTL	VCU385T	MTL	WYV50T	MTL	XLV146W	MTL
UKA23V	M I L	VCU386T	MTL	WYV52T	MTL	XLV147W	MTL
UNA763S	MTL	VCU387T	MTL	WYV58T	MTL	XLV148W	MTL
UNA776S	MTL	VCU389T	MTL	WYV59T	MTL	XLV149W	MTL
UNA788S	MTL	VCU390T	MTL	WYV61T	MTL	XLV150W	MTL
UPB301S	North Western	VCU391T	MTL	WYV65T	MTL	XLV151W	MTL
UPB308S	C M T	VCU392T	MTL	WYW9T	MTL	XLV152W	MTL
UPB309S	C M T	VCU393T	MTL	WYW12T	MTL	XLV153W	MTL
UPB317S	C M T	VCU394T	MTL	WYW25T	MTL	XLV154W	MTL
UPB322S	North Western	VCU395T	MTL	WYW26T	MTL	XLV155W	MTL
UPB334S	North Western	VCU396T	MTL	WYW27T	MTL	XLV156W	MTL
UPB335S	North Western	VCU397T	MTL	WYW32T	MTL	XLV157W	MTL
UPB342S	North Western	VCU398T	MTL	WYW33T	MTL	XLV158W	MTL
UPK125S	North Western	VCU399T	MTL	WYW35T	MTL	XLV159W	MTL
UPK137S	North Western	VCU401T	MTL	WYW42T	MTL	XLV160W	MTL
UPK138S	North Western	VCU402T	Village	WYW67T	MTL	XLV161W	MTL
UPK140S	North Western	VCU403T	MTL	WYW72T	MTL	XLV162W	MTL
UPK141S	North Western	VCU404T	MTL	WYW75T	MTL	XPG166T	North Western
USE434X	Ladyline	VCU405T	MTL	WYW78T	MTL	XPG169T	North Western
USO187S	Meredith	VDM937R	Bostock's	WYW79T	MTL	XPG171T	North Western
UTF119	Walkers	VJT606X	Bennett's	WYW80T	MTL	XPG177T	North Western
UTO3S	Huxley	VKB708	MTL	WYW81T	MTL	XPG181T	North Western
UTU550R	Bostock's	VKE561S	North Western	WYW82T	MTL	XPG193T	North Western
UTU551R	Bostock's	VLT268	MTL	WYW92T	MTL	XPT800V	Happy Al's
UTU980R	North Western	VPA150S	North Western	WYW95T	MTL	XRR129M	Walkers
UUM500R	Walkers	VRA124Y	Chester	XEM873W	MTL	XRR132M	Walkers
UWB534Y	Acorn Travel	VRA125Y	Chester	XEM874W	MTL	XRR133M	Walkers
UWW1X	Chester	VRG415T	MTL	XEM875W	MTL	XRR289S	Village
UWW2X	Chester	VRG416T	MTL	XEM876W	MTL	XRR291S	Village
UWW525L	Ladyline	VRG417T	MTL	XEM877W	MTL	XRR293S	Village
UWY81X	South Lancs	VRG418T	MTL	XEM878W	MTL	XRR294S	Village
VBG101V	MTL	VTB591L	Walkers	XEM879W	MTL	XRR295S	Village
VBG102V	MTL	VUA471X	Happy Al's	XEM880W	MTL	XRR296S	Village
VBG103V	MTL	WAG369X	Happy Al's	XEM881W	MTL	XTB5T	Warrington
VBG104V	MTL	WAG371X	Happy Al's	XEM882W	MTL	XTB6T	Warrington
VBG105V	MTL	WAG372X	Happy Al's	XEM883W	MTL	XTB7T	Warrington
VBG106V	MTL	WAG375X	Happy Al's	XEM884W	MTL	XTB8T	Warrington
VBG107V	MTL	WAG380X	Happy Al's	XEM885W	MTL	XTB9T	Warrington
VBG108V	MTL	WAG382X	Happy Al's	XEM886W	MTL	XTB10T	Warrington
VBG109V	MTL	WAW367	Meredith	XEM887W	MTL	XTB11T	Warrington
VBG110V	MTL	WCA941W	Bostock's	XEM888W	MTL	XYJ419	Acorn Travel
VBG111V	MTL	WCA942W	Bostock's	XEM889W	MTL	XYJ427	MTL
VBG112V	MTL	WCN643Y	MTL	XEM890W	MTL	YBN631V	Wingates
VBG113V	MTL	WDA914T	Village	XEM891W	MTL	YBN632V	Huxley
VBG114V	MTL	WGB869W	Nip-On	XEM892W	MTL	YCD72T	C M T
VBG115V	MTL	WLT446	MTL	XEM893W	MTL	YFY1M	North Western
VBG116V	MTL	WLT765	MTL	XEM894W	MTL	YMA99W	Chester
VBG117V	MTL	WLT912	MTL	XEM895W	MTL	YMA100W	Chester
VBG118V	MTL	WPT712R	C M T	XEM896W	MTL	YMA101W	Chester
VBG119V	MTL	WSU891	Wingates	XEM897W	MTL	YMA102W	Chester
VBG120V	MTL	WTU479W	North Western	XEM898W	MTL	YMA103W	Chester
VBG121V	MTL	WTU480W	North Western	XEM899W	MTL	YPL399T	North Western
VBG122V	MTL	WTU496W	North Western	XEM900W	MTL	YPL408T	North Western
VBG127V	MTL	WTU497W	North Western	XEM902W	MTL	YPL413T	C M T
VBG128V	MTL	WTU499W	North Western	XEM903W	MTL	YPL455T	North Western
VBG129V	MTL	WUH163T	Avon Buses	XEM904W	MTL	YSX931W	Nip-On
VBG130V	MTL	WVO856S	Lofty's	XEM905W	MTL	YTE587V	Merseyline
VBG133V	MTL	WWM907W	MTL	XEM906W	MTL	YTU983S	Halton
VCA453W	North Western	WWM908W	MTL	XEM907W	MTL	YTU986S	North Western
VCA454W	North Western	WWM909W	MTL	XEM908W	MTL	YWO182	Huxley
VCA455W	North Western	WWM910W	MTL				

British Bus Publishing

HANDBOOKS

Also available!

The Leyland Lynx - £8.95
The 1996 FirstBus Handbook - £9.95
The 1996 Stagecoach Bus Handbook - £9.95
The North East Bus Handbook - £9.95
The Yorkshire Bus Handbook - £9.95
The Lancashire, Cumbria & Manchester Bus Handbook - £9.95
The Scottish Bus Handbook - £9.95
The Welsh Bus Handbook - £9.95
The East Midlands Bus Handbook - £8.95
The South Midlands Bus Handbook - £8.95
The Model Bus Handbook - £9.95
The Fire Brigade Handbook - £8.95

Coming Soon

The North and West Midlands Bus Handbook - £9.95

Get the best!
Buy today from your transport bookshop,
or order direct from:

British Bus Publishing
The Vyne, 16 St Margaret's Drive, Wellington
Telford, Shropshire TF1 3PH
Fax and Credit Card orders: 01952 255669